P9-CCY-038

Thomas Hardy's
TESS OF THE D'URBERVILLES

Bloom's
NOTES

A CONTEMPORARY
LITERARY VIEWS BOOK

Edited and with an Introduction by
HAROLD BLOOM

MATIGNON HIGH SCHOOL LIBRARY
1 MATIGNON ROAD
CAMBRIDGE, MASS. 02140

823.8
Tho

© 1996 by Chelsea House Publishers, a division of Main Line Book Co.

Introduction © 1996 by Harold Bloom

All rights reserved. No part of this publication may be reproduced or transmitted in any form or by any means without the written permission of the publisher.

Printed and bound in the United States of America.

First Printing
1 3 5 7 9 8 6 4 2   /2/65

Cover Illustration: Archive Photo

Library of Congress Cataloging-in-Publication Data

Thomas Hardy's Tess of the d'Urbervilles / edited and with an introduction by Harold Bloom.
p. cm – (Bloom's notes)
Includes bibliographical references and index.
Summary: Includes a brief biography of the author, thematic and structural analysis of the work, critical views, and an index of themes and ideas.
ISBN 0-7910-4076-3
1. Hardy, Thomas, 1840–1928. Tess of the d'Urbervilles. [1. Hardy, Thomas. 1840–1928. Tess of the d'Urbervilles. 2. English literature— History and criticism.] I. Bloom, Harold. II. Series.
PR4748.T46 1995
823'.8—dc20
95-43494
CIP
AC

Chelsea House Publishers
1974 Sproul Road, Suite 400
P.O. Box 914
Broomall, PA 19008-0914

Contents

User's Guide

This volume is designed to present biographical, critical, and bibliographical information on Thomas Hardy and *Tess of the D'Urbervilles*. Following Harold Bloom's introduction, there appears a detailed biography of the author, discussing the major events in his life and his important literary works. Then follows a thematic and structural analysis of the work, in which significant themes, patterns, and motifs are traced. An annotated list of characters supplies brief information on the chief characters in the work.

A selection of critical extracts, derived from previously published material by leading critics, then follows. The extracts consist of such things as statements by the author on his work, early reviews of the work, and later evaluations down to the present day. The items are arranged chronologically by date of first publication. A bibliography of Hardy's writings (including a complete listing of books he wrote, cowrote, edited, or translated, along with important posthumous publications), a list of additional books and articles on him and on *Tess of the D'Urbervilles,* and an index of themes and ideas conclude the volume.

Harold Bloom is Sterling Professor of the Humanities at Yale University and Henry W. and Albert A. Berg Professor of English at the New York University Graduate School. He is the author of twenty books and the editor of more than thirty anthologies of literature and literary criticism.

Professor Bloom's works include *Shelley's Mythmaking* (1959), *The Visionary Company* (1961), *Blake's Apocalypse* (1963), *Yeats* (1970), *A Map of Misreading* (1975), *Kabbalah and Criticism* (1975), and *Agon: Towards a Theory of Revisionism* (1982). *The Anxiety of Influence* (1973) sets forth Professor Bloom's provocative theory of the literary relationships between the great writers and their predecessors. His most recent books are *The American Religion* (1992) and *The Western Canon* (1994).

Professor Bloom earned his Ph.D. from Yale University in 1955 and has served on the Yale faculty since then. He is a 1985 MacArthur Foundation Award recipient and served as the Charles Eliot Norton Professor of Poetry at Harvard University in 1987–88. He is currently the editor of the Chelsea House series Major Literary Characters and Modern Critical Views, and other Chelsea House series in literary criticism.

Introduction

HAROLD BLOOM

When I first read Hardy's novels, half a century ago, I liked (and still like) *The Woodlanders* best, but I understood why *The Return of the Native* was, at that time, the most popular of all of Hardy's major books. Today, *Tess of the D'Urbervilles* is the most read and studied of the novels, displacing even *The Mayor of Casterbridge,* the most overtly Shakespearean of Hardy's tragic visions. The universal popularity of *Tess of the D'Urbervilles* does not seem to me a feminist phenomenon; Sue Bridehead in *Jude the Obscure* ought to be far more of a feminist heroine. Virginia Woolf, who judged Hardy to be "the greatest tragic writer among English novelists," thought him also a master of "moments of vision," those Paterian bursts of radiance against a darkening background that served to enhance the infinite attractiveness of his heroines. I myself first fell in love with a literary character when, as a young boy, I was overwhelmed by the intensity of Marty South in *The Woodlanders.* I mention this not as part of my psychic biography but as a critical clue to the prevalence of *Tess of the D'Urbervilles* among us. Men and women, boys and girls, we fall in love with her, and we should, because Hardy was in love with her and presented her so as to cause us to emulate him.

In sociological or Marxist terms, Tess's tragedy is that of all of the English peasantry, and she cannot survive the dispersal of her class. Marxism, a Christian heresy, is massively irrelevant to Hardy, a firm Shelleyan atheist, and a believer in the philosopher Arthur Schopenhauer's remorseless Will-to-Live. Tess's erotic masochism is far more crucial to her tragedy than is any social exploitation that she undergoes. Increasingly, she convinces herself that she is a victim, and she finds in Stonehenge an appropriate context for her self-sacrificial impulses. In some ways, Tess was Hardy's Emma Bovary, since he seems to identify himself more with Tess than with anyone else among his many characters, even Jude in *Jude the Obscure.* While the novel is willing to ascribe a degree of masochistic culpability to Tess, essentially it represents her as the victim of a complex web of injustices. To render Tess tragic, Hardy knew that he had to ascribe a subtle complicity to Tess herself, for in order to be of tragic eminence (as she is), she had to limn her own night-piece, rather than consent to see it composed by her two unworthy lovers, Angel Clare and Alec D'Urberville.

Some feminist critics have condemned Hardy for projecting his own male fantasy in his eroticized portrait of Tess, whose taste for suffering can make all of us uncomfortable. That condemnation evades the high individuality of Tess; D. H. Lawrence emphasized the natural aristocrat in Tess, who "is passive out of self-acceptance, a true aristocratic quality, amounting almost to self-indifference." Lionel Johnson, Catholic poet and aesthete of the Nineties, loved Tess and her book but finally condemned her as lacking a proper capacity for spiritual transcendence:

> . . . the world was very strong; her conscience was blinded and bewildered; she did some things nobly, and some despairingly: but there is nothing, not even in studies of criminal anthropology or of morbid pathology, to suggest that she was wholly an irresponsible victim of her own temperament, and of adverse circumstances.

Was Johnson truly commenting upon the highly individual Tess, or upon John Webster's Duchess of Malfi or even Shakespeare's Cleopatra, Jacobean tragic heroines? Failed transcendence is as little relevant to the beautifully natural Tess as it would be to Cleopatra (despite her final, uncanny transcendence) or to the Duchess of Malfi. Tess is martyred because she is fully herself, a natural woman, but also because she (and Hardy) have a certain aesthetic taste for tragic suffering. ❖

Biography of Thomas Hardy

Thomas Hardy was born on June 2, 1840, in Higher Bockhampton, near Dorchester, England. His father, a mason, taught him to play the violin—they would often play together at country dances—and both his mother and grandmother passed on their love of books and stories to him. An avid student of Latin and history, Hardy became a Sunday school instructor at fifteen and planned to become a minister.

In 1856, the sixteen-year-old Hardy postponed his dream and became an architect's apprentice, relegating his studies of Latin, Greek, and the Bible to his spare time. After moving to London in 1862 to assist architect Arthur Blomfield, Hardy began writing as well. He won a prize for an 1863 essay on architecture and published the fictional "How I Built Myself a House" in *Chambers's Journal* in 1865. Reading Charles Darwin's scientific works caused him to doubt his faith, and he completely relinquished his notion of entering the church. Instead, he began composing poetry and submitting it to periodicals.

Hardy turned to writing prose soon after he returned home to recover from an illness in 1867. Still working in an architect's office, he wrote *The Poor Man and the Lady*. This novel, a satire on the nobility, was rejected for being too controversial and for lacking plot. In response to these criticisms, Hardy composed the elaborately plotted, melodramatic detective story *Desperate Remedies,* which was published in 1871.

As his writing career took off, his personal life underwent changes as well. In 1870, while planning the restoration of Cornwall's St. Juliot Church, Hardy met Emma Gifford, the rector's sister-in-law. Although he was already engaged to his cousin Tryphena Sparks, he fell in love with Gifford and married her in 1874. After Hardy's pastoral novel *Under the Greenwood Tree* debuted in 1872, Gifford encouraged him to give up architecture and concentrate on literature. She also assisted him by making a good copy of the romance *A Pair of Blue Eyes* (1873).

Shortly after the Hardys' wedding, *Far from the Madding Crowd* appeared in print. His first major work, the novel establishes Hardy's favorite southwestern English setting, the fictional Wessex. In tracing the saga of a woman learning the value of humble love after experiencing passionate but disastrous courtships, Hardy portrays rural life with drama, understanding, and humor. The novel achieved enough popularity for him to make a living as a writer, and he settled in London with his wife.

The couple traveled extensively, finally moving to a house in Sturminster Newton, where Hardy continued writing. The disappointing reaction to the social comedy *The Hand of Ethelberta* (1876) prompted Hardy to focus on the rural settings he knew best. *The Return of the Native* (1878) takes place in the desolate Egdon Heath in Wessex and dramatizes the misunderstandings and frustrations in a young woman's tragic life. His next three works also dealt with ill-fated romances: *The Trumpet-Major* (1880), *A Laodicean* (1881), and *Two on a Tower* (1882).

In 1883, Hardy moved to Dorchester, where he designed and built his home, Max Gate. The town inspired the setting for *The Mayor of Casterbridge* (1886), Hardy's next notable work. The novel depicts the downfall of a "man of character" through his impulsiveness and selfishness. The next year, Hardy published *The Woodlanders,* the story of an unhappily married woman and the marriage laws which restrict her. Over the next few years, he issued several collections of short stories, including *Wessex Tales* (1888), *A Group of Noble Dames* (1891), and *Life's Little Ironies* (1894).

As he grew bolder as an artist, Hardy roused some controversy. His accomplished novel *Tess of the D'Urbervilles* (1891) illuminates the cruel fate of "a pure woman" abused by men and further victimized by society's prudishness. The unusual portrayal of the heroine, a strong woman who continues trying to redeem her life until she is killed, earned the novel notoriety. *Jude the Obscure* (1896), the story of a man attempting to better himself through education only to be thwarted by the two women in his life, caused even more of a stir. With their critical depictions of sexuality, marriage, and Christian society, the two novels outraged many.

Deterred by the hostile reception of his work, Hardy stopped writing fiction after publishing the earlier serialized romance *The Well-Beloved* (1897). He returned to his first love, poetry, and published *Wessex Poems* in 1898; over the span of his life, he composed seven more volumes of verse, including *Satires of Circumstance* (1914), which tenderly recalled his courtship with his first wife, who died in 1912. Between 1904 and 1908, he also published a three-part epic drama of the Napoleonic war, *The Dynasts*. In 1914, Hardy married Florence Dugdale, a children's book author who had helped him with his research. His Arthurian drama *The Famous Tragedy of the Queen of Cornwall* was produced in 1923.

In his later years, Hardy was recognized as a gifted artist, receiving many honorary degrees and awards such as the gold medal of the Royal Society of Literature. He wrote an autobiography, which his wife published posthumously as a biography, *The Life of Thomas Hardy*. Hardy died on January 11, 1928. His heart was buried next to his first wife in Stinsford churchyard, but his ashes were placed in the Poets' Corner at Westminster Abbey. ❖

Thematic and Structural Analysis

Tess of the D'Urbervilles opens with incidents in rustic lives that, serving as symbols of fate and human helplessness, will motivate action throughout the novel (**Phase the First: The Maiden**). Jack Durbeyfield, a slightly drunken "haggler," walks home toward Marlott, in the Vale of Blackmoor, and meets a local parson who tells him he is a descendant of the once rich and noble d'Urbervilles, now extinct (**chapter one**). By this incongruous bit of history Durbeyfield, stretching prostrate among the daisies, comically fancies himself, thereafter, "Sir John." Names will often both designate and misrepresent appearances and origins, and coincidences are common and portentous. Sir John commands a passing boy to order him a carriage, and, as the first chapter closes, he hears distant music from the "women's walking club," the May Day Cerealia.

The Cerealia is a quaint local oddity. A debased ancient celebration of regeneration and renewal, it exists in the novel as a subtle emblem of vitality and loss. In this fertile and largely preindustrial agricultural valley, the mythic leaves a trace in such "metamorphosed or disguised form"; indeed, the supernatural permeates the natural world in the novel.

Durbeyfield's oldest daughter, Tess, is among the walkers and is embarrassed as her father rides past, boasting drunkenly of his "knighted forefathers" (**chapter two**). But at the same time, a young stranger of "superior class," named Angel, briefly joins the dancers. By the chance intrusion into Tess's world of unsought d'Urberville ancestry and a mute encounter with an unknown young man, the imagined promise of the past and the disguised cruelty of the future take their places in the narrative to reappear as ruthless instruments of fate.

Sixteen-year-old Tess Durbeyfield is a "vessel of emotion untinctured by experience." When Angel enters the May dance and fails to pick her as a partner, the narrator observes that she was indistinguishable from the others because "Norman blood" is, after all, of no consequence without "Victorian lucre." Hardy sets a tension between appearances and truth that the characters never resolve.¹ As Angel leaves, he regrets not having chosen her, and Tess feels the loss of something she cannot name. Her thoughts return to her father, and she walks home to the "yellow melancholy" of the Durbeyfields' "one-candled" cottage (**chapter three**). Meanwhile, her mother, Joan, thrilled by her husband's revelation of noble ancestry, has consulted a fortune-telling manual and suggests that Tess "claim kin" with a rich woman named d'Urberville at Trantridge, hopeful that marriage to a rich gentleman may result.

Jack Durbeyfield, who has been out celebrating his new nobility, cannot wake at two o'clock the next morning to take the beehives to market, so Tess and her young brother, Abraham, set out in the dark with the loaded wagon (**chapter four**). Abraham echoes their parents, imagining the improved fortunes of the family if Tess marries well. His thoughts wander to the sky, and he asks his sister whether they occupy a "splendid" or a "blighted" planet. "A blighted one," she responds. Her family's hopeless circumstances burden her with a sense of increasing responsibility toward the younger children. The novel's strongest theme is that external forces determine action and fate, and as brother and sister fall asleep on the moving wagon, their horse is run through by the shaft of an oncoming mail-cart and killed. The incident is crowded with foreshadowing allusions, omens of violent death and of Tess's culpability. Her father's livelihood is ruined without the horse, and Tess feels that she is a "murderess." She must now seek out Mrs. d'Urberville in order to help her family. Thus the parson's revelation in the first chapter names Tess's doom, and this crisis in the fourth chapter pushes her toward it.

In **chapter five** Tess arrives at the Trantridge d'Urbervilles' estate and meets Alec d'Urberville. She is struck by the "touches of barbarism" in his face and the absence of the "d'Urberville lineaments" she had somehow expected to find. She does not know that their claim to her ancestry is a work of imagination by a successful merchant, Alec's deceased father, to establish himself as a gentleman. Alec calls Tess "coz" and assumes a familiarity that makes her uncomfortable, but which she does not question. "Thus the thing began," remarks the narrator, "the thing" being the linking of circumstance and coincidence that will destroy both Tess and Alec. Tess is engaged to manage the fowl at the d'Urberville estate and formally leaves home, driven by the "capriciously passionate" Alec (**chapters six to nine**). "[I]t drank hard," the narrator tells us of the village of Trantridge (**chapter ten**). The monotony of Tess's daily occupation is relieved by weekly excursions to the local market town. A barn dance has a visible atmosphere of "vegeto-human pollen," the dust of peat and hay mixing with the warmth of the dancers. In the bacchanalian atmosphere they are "satyrs clasping nymphs—a multiplicity of Pans whirling a multiplicity of Syrinxes." Only Tess does not dance. In their lingering drunkenness on the walk home the revelers seem enveloped by a pagan relation to the world around them, "themselves and surrounding nature forming an organism of which all the parts harmoniously and joyously interpenetrated each other." But because of her experience at home, Tess has not drunk and is unimpressed by these effects of alcohol. The mood suddenly shifts as one of the women, a former "favourite" of Alec, drunkenly challenges Tess to a fight. Alec appears on horseback to rescue Tess, and the women laugh as the pair disappear into the woods. "Out of the frying-pan into the fire," one comments prophetically.

Alec now asks Tess why she continues to resist his kisses, and she tells him it is because she simply does not love him (**chapter eleven**). When he tells her he has given her father a new horse, her gratitude puts her at a further disadvantage, and, "inexpressibly weary," she begins to cry. Although Alec's rape of Tess is not clearly figured, the narrator's rhetorical questions point to the "immeasurable social chasm" that will now separate Tess from her earlier self, a girl whose experience had been "practically blank as snow." "[W]here was Tess's guardian angel? Where was the providence of her simple faith?" the narrator asks, answering in fatalistic words Joan Durbeyfield might use, " 'It was to be.' There lay the pity of it."

We do not immediately recognize Tess at the beginning of **chapter twelve (Phase the Second: Maiden No More)**. A woman struggles to carry a heavily laden basket, and we observe that the sensuous and innocent girl has been replaced by "a person who did not find her especial burden in material things." It is several weeks after the incident with Alec, and she walks toward home at Marlott having learned that "the serpent hisses where the sweet birds sing." Alec overtakes her and tries to persuade her to return with him. He is cold and impatient, partly concerned about the spectacle of misery she may present to her family, but he also shows traces of remorse, as if he knows no other course for himself. She refuses his offer of financial support.

Tess is next overtaken by a "text-painter" who offers to carry her basket. He stops to paint a Bible verse upon a stile (a sign post), words that seems to recognize and damn her. He is a moral idiot whose spiritual burlesque frightens Tess. She cannot believe that God ever said such cruel things as those the man paints: " 'I think they are horrible,' said Tess. 'Crushing! Killing!' " Much encouraged, he recommends the troubled girl to a parson, Mr. Clare, who is preaching that day in the vale. Caught between sensuous pagan intensity and a vague Christian idealism, Tess is in conflict with the "moral hobgoblins" of guilt and shame (**chapter thirteen**).

In **chapter fourteen** the August morning inspires a worship of visible phenomena. The sun is attentive and personal, a masculine "god-like creature" who returns the gaze of the earth. The modern world intrudes magnificently into the landscape: Like a heraldic symbol, the painted "Maltese Cross of the reaping-machine" appears as if "dipped in liquid fire." But the fantastic image is juxtaposed with a scene of common labor, the harvesters binding corn into sheaves. The machine symbolizes an indifferent and relentless fate as it cuts with "the teeth of the unerring reaper." It mindlessly drives the field's small animals into an ever narrower and more "ephemeral refuge" until, "huddled together, friends and foes," they are beaten and stoned to death by the harvesters. We cannot ignore the human parallel. Death is inevitable and life's persistence is embedded with doom.

At lunchtime Tess stops to nurse her baby in the field. That night, the child is deathly ill, and, with her small brother and sisters in attendance, Tess baptizes the dying baby. The narrator proclaims, "So passed away Sorrow the Undesired—that intrusive creature, that bastard gift of shameless Nature who respects not the social law." The episode is melodramatic but immensely moving.

· In **chapter fifteen** the burden of Tess's turbulent experiences intensifies to epiphany as she realizes that death will eventually obliterate the importance of all suffering. "But for the world's opinion those experiences would have been simply a liberal education," the narrator remarks, and even Tess muses that the "recuperative power that pervaded organic nature" might also reestablish her chastity. Nearly three years after the episode at Trantridge, Tess again leaves Marlott, now to become a milk-maid at Talbothay's dairy, some miles away from home and near estates that had once belonged to the ancient d'Urbervilles. Although Tess claims to want no "d'Urberville air-castles" in her dreams, she wonders if good fortune may come from the estates' nearness. Her "unexpended youth" still generates "hope, and the invincible instinct toward self-delight."

Chapter sixteen begins **Phase the Third: The Rally**, and as Tess approaches Talbothay's, nature seems to reflect her high spirits by "a pleasant voice in every breeze" and "joy" in the song of every bird. The dairyman, Mr. Crick, greets Tess, who begins milking at once (**chapter seventeen**). She recognizes a man, also engaged in milking, as the stranger who had joined the "walking-club" dance, and she hopes he does not recognize her. Tess learns that the young man is Angel Clare, the son of a parson, here to learn all he can about dairy work. Having rejected his father's Anglicanism, Angel studies to become a farmer.

· In **chapter eighteen** we understand Angel as a creature of high ideals and little passion who cherishes "intellectual liberty." But Angel comes down to earth, as it were, growing newly sensitive to the "moods" of the days and seasons, to the natural elements, and to the presence of Tess. He judges her a "fresh and virginal daughter of Nature" and thinks he may have seen her before, while into the dinner table conversation at the dairy a small image of doom intrudes as the dairyman holds his knife and fork erect on the table "like the beginning of a gallows." Angel's May Day appearance and now his reappearance, and the Reverend Clare's presence first through the text-painter and now through his son, together begin to frame Tess's fate.

The attraction between Tess and Angel grows in harmony with the seasons (**chapters nineteen to twenty-four**). Talbothay's is an idyllic place where poverty and dissatisfaction are absent and "natural feeling" thrives without social oppression. Tess and Angel are first to rise at the dairy and in the "aqueous light" of the midsummer daybreak feel as isolated as Adam and Eve. In these "non-human hours" he teasingly calls her by the names of pagan, natural goddesses. By July the Froom Vale is "oozing fatness and warm ferments" in the oppressive heat and Angel's passion for Tess has increased. He sneezes with repressed passion and, as Tess blushes, leaps forward from his milking stool to kiss her. She responds with the "unreflecting inevitableness" that is her greatest weakness.

Chapter twenty-five marks the beginning of **Phase the Fourth: The Consequence**. Unlike Alec d'Urberville, Angel Clare is "a man with a conscience," and the men seem clearly distinguished until both are revealed as destructively focused upon Tess. Alec's conscience is only activated after the fact, but Angel's extreme regard for Tess's virginity magnifies the destructive potential of both Tess's secret and Angel's scruples. He thinks that she would be a good wife to him in his vocation as a farmer, and he returns home to his father's vicarage to discuss the marriage—about which his parents are dubious. In **chapter twenty-six**, the Reverend Clare tells his son about his failure to persuade the locally notorious Alec d'Urberville from a life of "culpable passions"—which horrifies Angel—and so the fateful interweaving of reappearance and coincidence tightens around Tess.

Angel returns to the dairy and, in **chapters twenty-seven and twenty-eight**, tries to persuade Tess to marry him. He tells her of his father's encounter with a "young cynic," whom Tess recognizes as Alec. Despite her feelings of "grave hopelessness," her resistance weakens under the pressure of "two ardent hearts against one poor little conscience." She wonders why no one has told Angel of her relation to Alec and begins to think that marriage to Angel would be worth the risk of discovery. But, as if in warning—or anticipation—nature assumes grotesque aspects: The setting sun makes a "great forge in the heavens" as a "monstrous pumpkin-like moon" rises over willows tortured into "spiny-haired monsters."

After scrupulously and repeatedly refusing Angel, Tess finally accepts his proposal and writes to her mother. Joan Durbeyfield advises her daughter to say nothing of her "Bygone Trouble," so Tess resolves to try to dismiss her past. Her feelings of "indignation" toward men have changed to an "excess of honour" toward Angel Clare; his flaws only charm her. The narrator, however, is more circumspect and observes that Angel's love is "a fastidious emotion which could jealously guard the loved one against his very self." Tess wants to prolong their betrothal, keeping the wedding always something about to be, but Angel assures her that his feelings will never change and that she will never be without his "protection and sympathy" (**chapters twenty-nine to thirty-two**).

On Christmas Eve an ominous encounter with a Trantridge man who remembers her convinces Tess that she must, by letter if not by confrontation, tell Angel of her past (**chapter thirty-three**). She slips a letter under his door as he sleeps, and, when he makes no mention of it the next day, she hopes it means he has forgiven her. But New Year's Eve, the day before the wedding, arrives with Tess guiltily suspecting that Angel has not, in fact, read her letter; she discovers that she had inadvertently slipped it under the rug, where he never found it. She destroys it, and they proceed with the wedding. Immediately after, however, Tess is disturbed that their carriage seems unaccountably familiar—as if she had seen it in a dream. Angel suggests it may remind her of the well-known legend of the d'Urberville coach. She has not heard the story, and Angel knows only that a member of the family supposedly sees it before something happens. Tess wonders if her "idolatry" of Angel is dangerous, something "too desperate for human conditions." She fears that Alec may more rightfully be her husband. Ill omens abound and, as the chapter concludes, a cock crows three times.

Angel brings Tess to an ancient d'Urberville house, partially in ruins (**chapter thirty-four**). Two-hundred-year-old portraits of treacherous-looking women unmistakably resemble Tess.

Though Angel says nothing, he regrets having chosen this house. She puts on a jeweled necklace, bracelet, and earrings she has inherited from Angel's family and seems to him transformed into a fashionable woman of remarkable features. A man from the dairy arrives with their baggage and tells them that the cock's crowing had foretold "terrible affliction." Two milkmaids seem to have "gone out o' their minds": One has tried to drown herself, and the other was found "dead drunk" by a stand of willows. Tess knows that they had loved Angel and sadly watched him choose her. Believing that these innocent victims of "unrequited love" met an unhappy fate that should have been hers, she begins to tell Angel her secret. He interrupts, however, with a confession of his own, telling her that, for all his admiration of "spotlessness" and "purity," he had once spent forty-eight hours "in dissipation" with a woman. He asks Tess to forgive him. Much relieved, Tess trusts that he will find it easier to forgive her own failure because it is the mirror image of his. As she begins, however, the atmosphere of the room and her appearance become fantastic: The fire takes on a "Last Day luridness," reflected in the diamonds she wears like the "sinister wink[s]" of a toad.

Phase the Fifth: The Woman Pays opens as Tess awaits Angel's response to her confession. And now (**chapters thirty-five and thirty-six**) Tess begins to pay the penalty for what is, paradoxically, her social transgression. She asks Angel to forgive her, "in the name of love," as she has forgiven him for the same shame. But it is not the same: To him she has become "a species of imposter; a guilty woman in the guise of an innocent one." Wallowing in self-righteousness and imagined betrayal, he ignores her plea for mercy. He has sacrificed caste for "rustic innocence" and feels poorly rewarded. Tess, realizing that she cannot move him, offers to go home to Marlott. He quickly agrees. That night (**chapter thirty-seven**), Angel's distress is manifested in an incident of sleepwalking: He carries the still hopeful Tess to the ruins of an abbey, where he places her in an empty stone coffin. She carefully guides him back to the manor house without waking him. The next day, he seems to remember nothing of the incident, and she does not enlighten him. At a crossroads near Marlott they separate, with Angel telling her that, if he can someday endure her, he will come to her.

Meanwhile, she may write to his father if she is ill or in need of anything. Tess returns to her parents' home.

Eight months later Angel has sailed to Brazil and Tess has run out of money, but pride and shame prevent her from writing to Reverend Clare (**chapters thirty-eight to forty-one**). She contracts to work as a field laborer at Flintcomb-Ash, a hellish, "starve-acre place," where both sky and earth are "desolate drab" and outcroppings of "loose, white flints in bulbous, cusped, and phallic shapes" contrast with the fecund ripeness of the valleys (**chapters forty-two and forty-three**). The women appear to crawl over the field "like flies" as they "grub up" leafless turnips with a hooked fork; the winter is unusually cruel; and "gaunt spectral" birds from the polar regions come down into the fields to eat what the women may uncover.

In order to "stand or fall by her qualities" Tess has removed herself from both her husband's and her in-laws' lives. But in her desolation she decides to walk fifteen miles to the vicarage, introduce herself to the Reverend Clare and his wife, and inquire about her husband's well-being (**chapter forty-four**). If Angel's parents are as kind as he has told her, she reasons, they will help her "heart-starved" condition. She arrives at Emminster and, unrecognized, overhears Angel's brothers discussing the "ill-considered marriage" that has estranged him from them. Consumed with self-pity and convinced that they care as little for Angel as for her, she decides to return to Flintcomb-Ash without revealing herself to them. Then, passing through a village, she hears a preacher profess to have been "the greatest of sinners" until, through the words of a clergyman (Reverend Clare) and "the grace of Heaven," he had been changed. Tess is startled to discover that the preacher is Alec d'Urberville. **Chapter forty-five** begins **Phase the Sixth: The Convert** with a focus upon the energy and complexities of Alec d'Urberville. The irony of his "transfiguration" into a Methodist minister does not escape Tess, who remembers the persuasive rhetoric she had heard four years earlier. In Alec, "animalism had become fanaticism; Paganism Paulinism." He recognizes Tess as she turns to leave, and he overtakes her on the road, anxious to explain his conversion. She tells him of the pregnancy and child, and Alec is stunned. His shocking response is to make Tess take an oath, her hand upon what he thinks is an ancient Holy Cross, that she will never tempt him again. (She learns later that the stone is an unholy "thing of ill-omen.") Alec then follows Tess to Flintcomb-Ash and asks her to marry him (**chapter forty-six**). She tells him that she is already married, but refuses to reveal the identity of her husband. He asks what sort of husband would leave her in this place, and she responds too quickly, disclosing that he has left her because he found out about her past.

The threshing machine at which Tess works (**chapter forty-seven**) is a symbol of the bleak and impersonal machinations of fate, with even the engineman laboring "against his will in the service of his Plutonic master." Alec d'Urberville watches Tess feed wheat into the devouring machine and later confronts her as she eats her lunch. She asks why he continues to "trouble" her, and he parries that it is she who continues to trouble him. The "religious channel is left dry" in him by the information about their child, he claims, and all his feeling is now for her. She returns to the machine, and by **chapter forty-eight** her physical energy is almost gone. Tess can hardly speak as Alec, in the "seductive voice of the Trantridge time," tells her that his "religious mania" has been replaced by the desire to help her and her family. Her resistance to Alec is weakening, and that evening she writes her first letter to Angel Clare, begging him to give her some hope. "[C]ome to me, and save me from what threatens me," she pleads. She sends the letter to his father.

For Angel is still in Brazil, where he suffers the lingering effects of an illness he contracted shortly after his arrival (**chapter forty-nine**). Emotionally and spiritually he has aged, and life's pathos seems to have overwhelmed his rigid morality. Having forgotten his fierce command to Tess that she wait for him to contact her, he has been perplexed at her silence. Angel relates the events of his marriage to a "large minded," more worldly stranger whose perspective is more generous. The man tells him that Tess's past is of no importance compared to who she is and will be. This simple reduction of a problem Angel had thought a matter of deepest philosophy seems to release him and renew his love for Tess. In England, however,

Tess's burdens increase. She returns to Marlott (**chapter fifty**) when news reaches her that her parents are ill. Jack Durbeyfield subsequently dies, and the already impoverished family loses its lease on the cottage. On Old Lady Day, the "landless ones" prepare to join the others who migrate to new farms and new villages in hope of better fortune.

Alec d'Urberville interrupts Tess in a daydream in which she imagines she hears a carriage and horse (**chapter fifty-one**). Alec, who has arrived on horseback, tells her that the imaginary coach, a bad omen to the one who hears it, may be heard only by one of d'Urberville blood—and murder, either of or by the unlucky hearer, is its fulfillment. Of course, Alec cannot hear it. He inquires about her family's move and, declaring that Angel will never return to her, offers Tess and her family a cottage at Trantridge. Bewildered by Alec's kindness, Tess, for the first time, is roused by the injustice of Angel's coldness toward her. She sends a passionate letter accusing him of monstrous cruelty and tells him that she will try to forget him, as she and her family begin their migration (**chapter fifty-two**).

Phase the Seventh: Fulfilment opens as Angel returns to the vicarage, shocking his parents with his ravaged appearance and frailty. He reads Tess's last letter, despairs that she will never accept him, and soon leaves his parents' home to find her (**chapters fifty-three and fifty-four**). On his journey Angel passes the "unholy stone" on which Alec had made Tess swear, and the very nettles seem to mock nature's promise of renewal—and Angel's change of heart—as the "pale and blasted" stems of last year only generate more nettles. At Trantridge he finds Joan Durbeyfield, who tells him that Tess is at Sandbourne, where he arrives in **chapter fifty-five**.

Sandbourne is a "fashionable watering-place" of mansions and elegant people, an unlikely place for a milkmaid. Angel locates Tess at a "stylish lodging-house" and assumes, without blaming her, that she has sold the jewels. He holds his arms out to her and, when she makes no move toward him, assumes that his ravaged appearance repels her. He asks her to forgive him. "It is too late," she replies, her horror apparent only in her eyes, which shine "unnaturally." "Like a fugitive in a dream," she stands fixed and cries that she waited and wrote, yet he did not come. Alec has been kind to her and to her family and has "won [her] back to him." But, she goes on, becoming more agitated, Alec has lied, telling her that Angel would never come. She tells Angel to leave. Only later, we are told, does he realize that Tess was "a corpse upon a current" with no "living will."

Then, in a tone that was "a dirge rather than a soliloquy," Tess confronts Alec with her grief and accuses him of a most cruel betrayal (**chapter fifty-six**). She now believes that Angel, and not Alec, is her "own true husband," and that her "sin," while it allows her to live, is killing him. Underestimating the depth of her distress—although Tess writhes and has bitten her own lips to bleeding—Alec responds harshly. Moments later Tess calmly leaves the house, and only then, through the observations of the landlady, do we learn that Tess has stabbed Alec to death.

Walking out of Sandbourne, Angel is "broken in heart and numbed" (**chapter fifty-seven**). Tess runs after him to tell him she has killed Alec. "I owed it to you, and to myself, Angel," she explains; "It came to me in a shining light that I should get you back that way." Angel holds Tess tightly and tells her he loves her. He wonders if an inclination to murder might be part of her d'Urberville inheritance, or if the legend of the coach suggests that the family is predisposed to this kind of thing. In any event, this is his opportunity to make amends to Tess, and he does not fail her. They are like children in the immediacy of their affection and the scope of their plans. Angel guides them northward along obscure paths until they find an uninhabited, furnished mansion where they stay for five days, at last as husband and wife, speaking nothing of the time subsequent to their wedding (**chapter fifty-eight**). "All is trouble outside," Tess observes. By murdering Alec she has transgressed both social and natural law, and Angel knows her words are true, that "within was affection, union, error forgiven: outside was the inexorable."

When they sense that they have been discovered, they leave, Angel making a vague plan for their escape through some northern port. At midnight they arrive at a "monstrous" place Angel recognizes as Stonehenge. Dense clouds diffuse the moonlight as Angel and Tess move among the giant pillars, and the wind "hums" as if through a one-stringed harp. Tess, who can walk no farther, lies upon a stone slab that Angel then realizes is an altar. She reminds him that he called her a heathen at Talbothay's, so now she is home. She demands nothing more except that Angel marry her younger sister, that he "bring her up for [his] own self" in order to keep her spirit somehow alive and always with him. Angel watches over her as she sleeps. The police find them, and all wait quietly for Tess to wake. "I shall not live for you to despise me," she tells him, as she rises to meet her fate.

In the **final chapter**, Angel Clare and his sister-in-law, a "spiritualized image of Tess," watch the raising of a black flag over the tower of the prison, signaling that Tess is hanged. The narrator proposes an overarching pagan theme to frame the cruelty of Tess's fate: " 'Justice' was done, and the President of the Immortals, in Aeschylean phrase, had ended his sport with Tess." Nature's regeneration and renewal suggest both a promise and a sentence of doom. Justice is a sublunary delusion. ✤

—*Tenley Williams*
New York University

List of Characters

Tess Durbeyfield is sixteen years old when the novel begins and twenty-one at its conclusion; her innocence and victimization suggest that she is Hardy's reproach to Victorian ideals of chastity. Her inept parents are rustic "cottagers," poor even in a rural village. Tess, however, has a finer sensibility that ennobles her. By a pagan relation to nature mixed with a "vague Christian idealism," she lives in her body and the natural world, translating everything through her feelings and senses, but with an innate code of responsibility and rightness. Her relation to nature often seems reciprocal: Lushness surrounds her at Talbothay's as she recovers from her rape by Alec d'Urberville; a hellish barrenness characterizes Flintcomb-Ash after Angel Clare abandons her. Tess is destroyed more by the social crime of lost virginity than by the act of rape itself. And, with the death of the child, her sin becomes a secret outside of nature, society's killing blight against what Hardy calls "a pure woman."

Tess is highly moral in the sense that she does not squander her affection. She believes in the purity of Angel's ideals and in the efficacy of her love until convinced that he has abandoned her. When Angel finds her with Alec at Sandbourne, she is emotionally dead, living with the man she believes should have been her husband. Her love for Angel revives, but her choice is irrevocable. Social law can never accommodate Tess and Angel. Though Tess's sanity is suspect when she kills Alec, her strength to act is as noble as it is heartbreaking. The egoism of both men has trapped her within social strictures she can never escape. She returns to Angel, and, for a little while, they are outlaws absorbed by their love for each other.

Alec d'Urberville is a counterfeit d'Urberville. His family has taken the name of an extinct nobility whose only survivors are the Durbeyfields. Coarse-featured, callous, and sensual, he assumes physical power over Tess when she is weary and unable to resist. The rape is unconscionable, as is his demand that Tess swear never to tempt him again, but Hardy does not depict a monster. Alec is instead an extreme portrait of male power over innocence; he seems to have no choice but to be as he is, and he begins to love Tess because she is unlike him. He offers financial support in compensation for the rape and cannot understand her sensitivity. Once he has acquired religion and the form of a conscience, and has learned of the child, he offers marriage. But after Tess tells him she is already married, and after she persuades him from his religious enthusiasm with Angel's logical arguments, he pursues her relentlessly until she submits to him. Alec is a creature of will who wins Tess, in a sense, after she is already dead. She is only able to again know pure feeling and briefly retrieve Angel's love by stabbing Alec as he, figuratively, stabbed her.

Angel Clare, like Alec, is a creature of will, but his takes the hue of moral and mental conviction. A lover of "intellectual liberty," he rejects his father's Anglicanism in favor of ideals such as "purity"—but, sadly, his ideals do not include the compassion that inspires his father's beliefs. While Alec rapes Tess physically, Angel rapes her emotionally, and they are equally brutal. Angel leaves Tess after their wedding, unable to "endure" her confession about her past. Self-righteous and self-absorbed, he is all intellect and injury as he pitilessly abandons her. When he finally comes for her, his love more mature, he is too late. After the murder he returns the love she gives without restraint, but he still seems unworthy. "Tenderness was absolutely dominant in Clare at last," and he cannot fail her because there is no future.

Jack Durbeyfield is the first character we meet and the first to learn of his d'Urberville heritage, whereupon he imagines himself "Sir John." He is a tipsy and abstracted patriarch whose gender alone ironically supersedes his weaknesses, to the continual misfortune of his family. Although neither wealthy nor intellectual, he is, like Alec and Angel, a portrait of male power. His wife Joan accepts him as he is, and to Tess he is an unopposable nuisance. As her father seems less and less capable of protecting his family, Tess feels an increasing responsibility for her younger siblings that pushes her toward doom. Jack, by no volition of his own, is vested in death with a terrible legal power as the leasehold on the family cottage ends with him. Joan, Tess, and the children are left homeless and destitute, and Tess has no choice but to accept Alec on his terms.

Joan Durbeyfield, Tess's mother, is a good-natured, childlike woman whose love for her oldest daughter is as ineffectual as it is unconditional. Absorbed in childrearing and a slovenly domesticity, her life's refrain is that she can never get the wash done. Tess applies to her for advice and direction, and her mother fails her in every instance. Tess cannot hear the grim folk-wisdom embedded in the popular songs her mother loves to sing, yet Joan cannot dispense this wisdom in any other way. Superstitious and a believer in fortune-telling, Joan is also a fatalist who accepts poverty, family disgrace, Tess's ruin, her husband's death, and losing her home, all with a sense of inevitability. Tess and her mother compare as if "the Jacobean and the Victorian ages were juxtaposed." ❖

Critical Views

[Margaret Oliphant (1828–1897) was a prolific Scottish novelist and essayist. Among her critical works is the noted *Literary History of England* (1882). In this review of *Tess of the D'Urbervilles,* Oliphant admires the novel but takes offense at what she believes is Hardy's portrayal of vice under the guise of virtue in the character of Tess.]

We have not a word to say against the force and passion of this story. It is far finer in our opinion than anything Mr. Hardy has ever done before. The character of Tess up to her last downfall, with the curious exceptions we have pointed out, is consistent enough, and we do not object to the defiant blazon of a Pure Woman, notwithstanding the early stain. But a Pure Woman is not betrayed into fine living and fine clothes as the mistress of her seducer by any stress of poverty or misery; and Tess was a skilled labourer, for whom it is very rare that nothing can be found to do. Here the elaborate and indignant plea for Vice, that it is really Virtue, breaks down altogether. We do not for a moment believe that Tess would have done it. Her creator has forced the *rôle* upon her, as he thinks (or says) that the God whom he does not believe in, does—which ought to make him a little more humble, since he cannot, it appears, do better himself. But whatever Mr. Hardy says, we repeat that we do not believe him. The lodgings at the seaside, drawing-room floor; 'the rich cashmere dressing-gown of grey white, embroidered in half mourning tints'; 'the walking costume of a well-to-do young lady', with a veil over her black hat and feathers; her 'silk stockings' and 'ivory parasol',—are not the accessories of purity, but the trappings of vice. Tess would have flung them out of the window. She would not have stabbed Mr. Alec D'Urberville, her potential husband, with the carving-knife intended for the cold ham (which, besides, awakens all sorts of questions, as—why did Alec D'Urberville, a strong young man, allow himself to be stabbed? and how did it happen that the lodging-house carving-knife, not usually a very sharp instrument, was capable of such a blow?), but have turned him head and shoulders out of the poorest cottage in which he had insulted her with such a proposition. It is no use making men and women for us, and then forcing them to do the last thing possible to their nature. If Tess did this, then Tess, after all her developments, was at twenty a much inferior creature to the unawakened Tess at sixteen who would not live upon the wages of iniquity; and thus two volumes of analysis and experience are lost, and the end is worse than the beginning—which, after watching Tess through these two volumes, and following the progress of her thoughts much more articulately than she could have done herself, we absolutely decline to believe. Whoever that person was who went straight from the endearments of Alec D'Urberville to those of the Clare Angel or the Angel Clare, whatever the image is called, Mr. Hardy must excuse us for saying pointedly and firmly that she was not Tess; neither was she a Pure Woman. This is the portion of the book which was served up to keen appetites in the Reviews, and we rejoice to think that it was so. Let the cultivated reader keep the nastiness for which it seems he longs. We are delighted to find ourselves on the side of the honest lover of a story who requires no strong stimulation of criminality thrown in against all the possibilities of natural life.

—Margaret Oliphant, [Review of *Tess of the D'Urbervilles*], *Blackwood's Edinburgh Magazine* 151, No. 3 (March 1892): 473–74

❖

LIONEL JOHNSON ON THE STRUGGLE AGAINST CONVENTION IN *TESS OF THE D'URBERVILLES*

[Lionel Johnson (1867–1902) was a well-known British poet of his generation as well as a literary critic and reviewer. His critical works have been gathered in *Post Liminium* (1911) and *Reviews and Critical Papers* (1921). In this extract from *The Art of Thomas Hardy* (1894), Johnson examines the personal and social changes presented in *Tess of the D'Urbervilles*.]

Tess was changing from peasant ignorance and convention, when she met Clare, changing from the conventional culture and belief of a higher station; the woman struggling up from superstition, the man struggling free from prejudice: the two natures, breaking with the past, came together, she straining towards his level of thought, he stooping to her level of life: the result was a tragic discord. It might be interpreted in many ways. Perhaps the superstitious faith of the Durbeyfield household, and the Calvinist faith of the Clare household, were more nearly in accord with the essential verities of life, than the new aims and impulses of their offspring: perhaps Tess and Clare carried right theories into wrong practice: perhaps one alone did so: certainly, we have in this story a singular presentation of the struggle between old and new, in various ranks of life and ranges of thought; of the contact of the new in one rank and range with the new in another; of the curious reversion, in each case, of the new to the old. Tess acts, on several occasions, from impulses and in ways, which derive, so her maker hints, from her knightly ancestors: Clare, at the crisis of her life and of his own, falls back in cruel cowardice to the conventional standards of that society, which he so greatly scorns. Tess, again, having learned by ear and heart Clare's arguments against Christian theology, repeats them to her old betrayer, Alec D'Urberville, then a fanatical convert to the Calvinism of Clare's father: and she enables him thereby to become a second time her betrayer. Finally, this tangled play of new things upon old comes to its wretched end at Stonehenge, the most ancient of religious monuments in England, and at Winchester, the ancient capital of England: religion, however stern, society, however cruel, are vindicated in the presence of their august memorials. The old, we are meant to feel, was wrong, and the new was right: but the inhuman irony of fate turned all to misunderstanding and to despair: the new devil quoted the new scriptures in the ears of the new believers; and they went to the old destruction.

—Lionel Johnson, *The Art of Thomas Hardy* (London: Elkin Mathews; New York: Dodd, Mead, 1894), pp. 175–76

❖

[Lascelles Abercrombie (1881–1938) was an eminent British man of letters, journalist, poet, and lecturer. His critical works include *The Theory of Poetry* (1926), *Romanticism* (1926), and *Principles of Literary Criticism* (1932). In this extract, Abercrombie comments on the character and function of Angel Clare.]

Angel Clare is the one figure in the book who is at all out of the ordinary run of human nature. His squeamish, fastidious nature, conscious of his own purity and unconscious of his deep insincerity, mixing with farm-hands as an equal and always feeling his own superiority, pretentiously broad-minded and essentially mean, is analysed with considerable care. He is not so pushed forward as to be too noticeable, however; though he is undoubtedly real enough to be odious. In fact, he is the only one of Hardy's characters who is genuinely odious. Even if one knew all about Alec D'Urberville, one could bear to have dinner with him; yes, and even those starched ninnyhammers, Angel's two parsonical brothers, might be agreeably talked to at a garden party. But no decent person, knowing Angel's history, would house with him or, if possible, talk with him. For he is theoretical high-mindedness; and than this there is nothing more disgusting, let alone its cruelty when it gets any actual life into its power. He, and not her seducer, is the real poison in Tess's life. Whether, when the story ends, he is to marry 'Liza-Lu, is not quite clear; Hardy seems to have shrunk from definitely adding to the sorrow of the book's close a piece of tragic irony similar to the comic irony with which The Alchemist ends. But I am sure he does marry her, and generously trains her to his standards; I am sure, at any rate, that the rest of his life is not much tormented with the pangs of self-contempt. Yet Angel Clare is profoundly necessary to the whole art of the book. If, for the sake of a moment's convenience, we allow ourselves roughly to allegorize the story, then Tess will be the inmost purity of human life, the longing for purity which has its intensest instinct in virginity; and Alec D'Urberville is "the measureless grossness and the slag" which inevitably takes hold of life, however virginal its desires. That is bad enough; it is a type of the fundamental tragedy of life. But the tragedy could be endured. It is Angel Clare who turns it to unendurable agony; for he is the venom not so much of self-consciousness as of introspection, horribly exaggerating the tragedy, adding that dreadful element, the idea of remorse, taking enforced impurity as a personal sin, cruelly *blaming* life for that the helpless fact of its existence does not equal its desires. And introspection is a no less essential part of the whole human tragedy, as this book has to declare it, than anything else therein.

—Lascelles Abercrombie, *Thomas Hardy: A Critical Study* (London: Martin Secker, 1912), pp. 107–9

❖

D. H. LAWRENCE ON ALEC D'URBERVILLE AND ANGEL CLARE

[D. H. Lawrence (1885–1930), the celebrated British novelist and poet, was also an astute if idiosyncratic critic. Among his critical works are *Movements in European History* (1921), *Fantasia of the Unconscious* (1922), and the celebrated *Studies in Classic American Literature* (1923). In this extract from a long essay on Hardy written in 1914 but published only posthumously, Lawrence contrasts the characters of Alec D'Urberville and Angel Clare, both of whom are flawed because they do not unify the male and female aspects of human character.]

Tess never tries to alter or to change anybody, neither to alter nor to change nor to divert. What another person decides, that is his decision. She respects utterly the other's right to be. She is herself always.

But the others do not respect her right to be. Alec d'Urberville sees her as the embodied fulfilment of his own desire: something, that is, belonging to him. She cannot, in his conception, exist apart from him nor have any being apart from his being. For she is the embodiment of his desire.

This is very natural and common in men, this attitude to the world. But in Alec d'Urberville it applies only to the woman of his desire. He cares only for her. Such a man adheres to the female like a parasite.

It is a male quality to resolve a purpose to its fulfilment. It is the male quality, to seek the motive power in the female, and to convey this to a fulfilment; to receive some impulse into his senses, and to transmit it into expression.

Alec d'Urberville does not do this. He is male enough, in his way; but only physically male. He is constitutionally an enemy of the principle of self-subordination, which principle is inherent in every man. It is this principle which makes a man, a true male, see his job through, at no matter what cost. A man is strictly only himself when he is fulfilling some purpose he has conceived: so that the principle is not of self-subordination, but of continuity, of development. Only when insisted on, as in Christianity, does it become self-sacrifice. And this resistance to self-sacrifice on Alec d'Urberville's part does not make him an individualist, an egoist, but rather a nonindividual, an incomplete, almost a fragmentary thing.

There seems to be in d'Urberville an inherent antagonism to any progression in himself. Yet he seeks with all his power for the source of stimulus in woman. He takes the deep impulse from the female. In this he is exceptional. No ordinary man could really have betrayed Tess. Even if she had had an illegitimate child to another man, to Angel Clare, for example, it would not have shattered her as did her connexion with Alec d'Urberville. For Alec d'Urberville could reach some of the real sources of the female in a woman, and draw from them. Troy could also do this. And, as a woman instinctively knows, such men are rare. Therefore they have a power over a woman. They draw from the depth of her being.

And what they draw, they betray. With a natural male, what he draws from the source of the female, the impulse he receives from the source he transmits through his own being into utterance, motion, action, expression. But Troy and Alec d'Urberville, what they received they knew only as gratification in the senses; some perverse will prevented them from submitting to it, from becoming instrumental to it.

Which was why Tess was shattered by Alec d'Urberville, and why she murdered him in the end. The murder is badly done, altogether the book is botched, owing to the way of thinking in the author, owing to the weak yet obstinate theory of being. Nevertheless, the murder is true, the whole book is true, in its conception.

Angel Clare has the very opposite qualities to those of Alec d'Urberville. To the latter, the female in himself is the only part of himself he will acknowledge: the body, the senses, that which he shares with the female, which the female shares with him. To Angel Clare, the female in himself is detestable, the body, the senses, that which he will share with a woman, is held degraded. What he wants really is to receive the female impulse other than through the body. But his thinking has made him criticize Christianity, his deeper instinct has forbidden him to deny his body any further, a deadlock in his own being, which denies him any purpose, so that he must take to hand, labour out of sheer impotence to resolve himself, drives him unwillingly to woman. But he must see her only as the Female Principle, he cannot bear to see her as the Woman in the Body. Her he thinks degraded. To marry her, to have a physical marriage with her, he must overcome all his ascetic revulsion, he must, in his own mind, put off his own divinity, his pure maleness, his singleness, his pure completeness, and descend to the heated welter of the flesh. It is objectionable to him. Yet his body, his life, is too strong for him.

Who is he, that he shall be pure male, and deny the existence of the female? This is the question the Creator asks of him. Is then the male the exclusive whole of life?—is he even the higher or supreme part of life? Angel Clare thinks so: as Christ thought.

Yet it is not so, as even Angel Clare must find out. Life, that is Two-in-One, Male and Female. Nor is either part greater than the other.

—D. H. Lawrence, "Study of Thomas Hardy" (1914), *Phoenix: The Posthumous Papers of D. H. Lawrence,* ed. Edward D. McDonald (New York: Viking, 1936), pp. 483–85

❖

[William R. Rutland was a literary scholar who wrote
Swinburne: A Nineteenth Century Hellene (1931) and
*Thomas Hardy: A Study of His Writings and Their
Background* (1938), from which the following extract is
taken. Here, Rutland argues that Hardy's muddled
indictment of human society renders *Tess* a flawed
tragedy.]

In so far as it voices a grievance against human society, *Tess* is
a failure. As ⟨Lionel⟩ Johnson showed, the indictment lacks
both coherence and consistency; moreover, Hardy did not
even clearly make up his mind what it was that he was indict-
ing. He struck out wildly, but he hit nothing. Now he attacks
human society for framing laws and conventions which run
counter to Nature; and now he cries out against the cruelty of
universal Nature, in whose breasts there runs none of the milk
of human kindness. The famous passages have become hackneyed: had Tess been alone on a desert island, she would not
have been wretched; her baby is 'that bastard gift of shameless
Nature who respects not the social law'; her misery is 'based
on nothing more tangible than a sense of condemnation under
an arbitrary law of society which had no foundation in nature';
but for social conventions, her experience would have been
simply a liberal education; and so on. What has to be said
about this part of the argument in *Tess* is not, as the many who
have so enthusiastically hailed Hardy as a great prophet, claim,
that it is true; for it is not even convincing; but that it is something which developed very late in Hardy's art, flamed up
fiercely for a little while, and then died out altogether. This
indictment of human society is not to be found in *The Return of
the Native,* except by the prejudice which sees what it desires
to see; it is hardly to be discovered in the *Dynasts.*

With the other part of the argument in *Tess,* the matter is
very different. Here, the passages are more numerous, and
equally hackneyed. Before the story is well started, Hardy
describes the Durbeyfield family and demands indignantly
where Wordsworth gets his authority for speaking of 'Nature's
holy plan.' Tess is made to tell her little brother that we live on

a blighted world. There is the outburst against 'a morality good enough for divinities but scorned by average human nature.' 'In the ill-judged execution of the well-judged plan of things . . . Nature does not often say "See!" to her poor creature at a time when seeing can lead to happy doing.' Angel Clare asks Tess: 'This hobble of being alive is rather serious, don't you think so?' Tess could hear in the words of M. Sully Prud'homme (which, by the way, she would certainly not have understood) a penal sentence in the fiat: 'Tu naîtras.' Tess found in the 'Ode on Intimations of Immortality' a ghastly satire, for: 'to her and her like, birth itself was an ordeal of degrading personal compulsion whose gratuitousness nothing in the result seemed to justify.' And so forth. Considered as literature, there was nothing new in all this, as some of the most fervid admirers of *Tess* seemed to think. ⟨. . .⟩

What should be said about such passages is not, as too many would-be critics have said, that they are true; for the question of their truth can never be taken to a higher court of appeal than personal views of life; but that they are the culmination of Hardy's spiritual development during thirty years, at least. When Tess thinks that all is vanity, we are told that she thought further: 'If all were only vanity, who would mind it? All was, alas, worse than vanity—injustice, punishment, exaction, death.' Nearly twenty years before he wrote those words in the novel, Hardy had written in his private diary:

> 'All is vanity,' saith the Preacher. But if all were only vanity, who would mind? Alas, it is too often worse than vanity; agony, darkness, death also. A man would never laugh were he not to forget his situation, or were he not one who has never learnt it.

In the interval, Hardy had undergone the influences outlined in an earlier chapter, and his views had darkened as the years passed over him. The older he grew, the more ghastly a business the universe seemed to him to be. ⟨. . .⟩

Tess of the d'Urbervilles is a tragedy. It was laid down long ago by Aristotle, in the fourteenth chapter of the *Poetics,* that the object of tragedy in the form of drama is to produce terror and pity, τὸ φοβερὸν καὶ ἐλεεινὸν. 'The plot,' he says, 'should be so constructed that even without seeing the play anyone hearing of the incidents thrills with fear and pity as a result of what occurs.' Although this was written about plays, it has generally been accepted as applicable to all imaginative tragedies in literature. It is certainly true of *The Mayor of Casterbridge*. But in *Tess*, Hardy has endeavoured to provide the element of terror, less in the substance of the story itself than in the background to it; which may be called argumentative, theological, dogmatic, philosophical or what you will, but which is not intrinsic to the picture. In so far as it is not intrinsic, the book falls short of the highest artistic standards. Judged by another famous theory of tragedy, the theory that tragedy lies, not in the conflict of right with wrong, but in the conflict of right with right, the same conclusion must be reached; for in *Tess* all Hardy's powers are put forth to make us feel the right on one side only.

—William R. Rutland, *Thomas Hardy: A Study of His Writings and Their Background* (Oxford: Basil Blackwell, 1938), pp. 230–34

❖

EDMUND BLUNDEN ON HARDY'S NOTIONS OF THE "PURITY" OF TESS

[Edmund Blunden (1896–1974) was a noted British poet who lectured both in Tokyo and at Oxford University. His critical works include *Shelley: A Life Story* (1947), *War Poets 1914–1918)* (1958), and *John Clare: Beginner's Luck* (1971). In this extract, Blunden recalls some discussions with Hardy on his conception of Tess's "purity."]

Hardy agreed that he was sometimes described as the novelist of the agricultural labourer, but with his usual dryness commented, "That is not inclusive, I think." Conversation naturally found its way to his latest book, and gave him the cue to tell a pretty story of a village girl who had lately retorted to his compliments on her good looks with "Ah, but you don't think me so nice as Tess." Hardy replied, "But she isn't real; you are." "What!" said the girl. "Oh, I thought she lived in that house over the hill there." She was much relieved, Hardy gathered, to know that Tess was no practical rival.

Questioned further about his book, Hardy admitted that he was sorry not to have been able to rescue Tess at the last, as so many had hoped, but so it had to be. "You must have felt it a pain to bring her to so fearful an end." "Yes. Such dreams are we made of that I often think of the day when, having decided that she must die, I went purposely to Stonehenge to study the spot. It was a gloomy lowering day, and the skies almost seemed to touch the pillars of the great heathen temple." As for "a pure woman", it was suggested that Tess's first love-trouble did not deprive her of that name, but that "her absolutely unnecessary return to Alec d'Urberville" did; to that Hardy replied, "But I still maintain that her innate purity remained intact to the very last; though I frankly own that a certain outward purity left her on her last fall. I regarded her then as being in the hands of circumstances, not normally responsible, a mere corpse drifting with a current to her end." When it was forecast that the broad result of the book would be a greater freedom for open and serious discussion of some deep problems of human life, Hardy went slow. (He had of course no desire to set himself up as a protagonist in the manner of W. T. Stead.) "That would be a very ambitious hope on my part. Remember I am only a learner in the art of novel-writing. Still I do feel very strongly that the position of man and woman in nature may be taken up and treated frankly."

—Edmund Blunden, *Thomas Hardy* (London: Macmillan, 1941), pp. 78–80

❖

DAVID CECIL ON SOME PLOT ELEMENTS IN *TESS OF THE D'URBERVILLES*

[Lord David Cecil (1902–1986) was a lecturer at Oxford University and an important critic and biographer. He wrote *Early Victorian Novelists* (1935), *Poets and Story-Tellers* (1949), and *Walter Pater: The Scholar-Artist*

(1955). In this extract from his book on Hardy, Cecil examines some elements of the plot in *Tess,* particularly the triangle of Alec, Tess, and Angel.]

It is essential to the development of his plot that Alec should get Tess into his clutches again after she has been deserted by Angel. But how is this going to be managed? For Tess had never liked Alec and now hated him as the author of all her woes. Indeed, he has been presented to us—in so far as he has any individuality at all—as a cigar-smoking, rich young vulgarian, living only for his own animal pleasure. Hardy, however, suddenly reintroduces him into the book in the unexpected character of a Revivalist preacher. Alec, he tells us, has been converted. Far be it from me to deny that pleasure-loving vulgarians can undergo religious conversions. But the event is too odd for the reader to be expected to accept it without explanation. Alec should have been described to us as possessing some emotional streak in his disposition which might make such an occurrence probable. Hardy never attempts to do this: indeed, when, once more for the purposes of the plot, Alec has to behave like a villain again, Hardy simply says airily that his conversion lost its power and that he has reverted to what he was before. All through his books, the reader is liable to knock up against these crude pieces of machinery, tearing the delicate fabric of imaginative illusion in tatters.

The novelist has not finished his task when he has reconciled form with fact. His second problem is to reconcile fact with imagination. He has to give a convincing impression of the real world, but he has also to express his personal vision. And he only achieves complete success in his art if he satisfies both these conditions equally. This is an even harder problem. Many distinguished novelists have never achieved it. *Women in Love* blazes with the fire of Lawrence's temperament. But as a picture of county society in twentieth-century England it is—to say the least of it—far-fetched. Gissing, on the other hand, gives us a most reliable record of the life of the serious-minded poor in Victorian London. But it is only intermittently tinged with an individual colour. Hardy is no more successful than these eminent authors. He errs, as we might expect, with Lawrence rather than with Gissing. His creative power is so much stronger than his critical sense that he always disregards probability if it stands in the way of the emotional impression he wishes to make. As a matter of fact, he was not a good judge of probability.

—David Cecil, *Hardy the Novelist: An Essay in Criticism* (Indianapolis: Bobbs-Merrill, 1943), pp. 165–67

❖

Harvey Curtis Webster on Hardy's Social Views

[Harvey Curtis Webster (b. 1906) was formerly a professor of English at the University of Louisville. He is the author of *After the Trauma: Representative British Novelists Since 1920* (1970) and *On a Darkling Plain: The Art and Thought of Thomas Hardy* (1947), from which the following extract is taken. Here, Webster argues that *Tess* is an illustration of the pessimistic view of society found in much of Hardy's work.]

Hardy's avowed intention in *Tess of the D'Urbervilles* (1891) was to present a story in which the conventions would be so reversed that a seduced girl becomes the heroine. If this true sequence of events should offend some, he asks that they remember that it is better that an offense should come out of the truth than that the truth should not be told. From Hardy's defensive attitude in this Preface to the work, one assumes that he is about to attack society more wholeheartedly than he has done before—an assumption that the book as a whole confirms. But *Tess* nonetheless illustrates the "pessimistic" view of the world that has frequently been assumed to be *the* philosophy of the Wessex novels.

The characters and the author stress the magnipotence of Fate. Izz, Marion, and Retty do not blame Tess for winning the man they love. 'Twas to be. Although she was at first inclined to believe herself mistress of her fate, Tess soon begins to admit the fatalistic convictions of the neighboring field folk, who associate more with natural phenomena than with man. One of these field folk, her mother, looks upon Tess's seduction with a fatalism similar to that with which she regards the weather. Sometimes the characters are still more specific in their statements of belief. Tess refuses to pray for Alec because she realizes that the great Power would not alter his plans on her account. She feels that the universe is an "immense sad soul, coterminous with the universe in space, with history in time." Angel Clare speaks of Tess's life as the only chance given her by an "unsympathetic First Cause." But it is Hardy himself who most clearly and often specifies the nature of the controlling power.

The most memorable of these specifications is, of course, the ironical sentence, " 'Justice' was done, and the President of the Immortals, in Aeschylean phrase, had ended his sport with Tess." But this is really no more than a trope, indicative of the way the fate of Tess impresses unreasoning humanity. Hardy's more seriously intended statements are frequently addressed against conceptions that are conventional rather than statements of a new force such as we know he had conceived of. Where, Hardy asks, was the providence of Tess's simple faith when she was seduced? What justice satisfactory to man can be found in the retribution that offers up Tess as a sacrifice for the sins of her ancestors? After he had described the utter dependence of the D'Urbeyfield children upon their improvident parents, he says: "Some people would like to know whence the poet whose philosophy is in these days deemed as profound and trustworthy as his song is breezy and pure gets his authority for speaking of 'Nature's holy plan.' " More positively, Hardy speaks of his sympathy with the fatalism of the peasants, the unalterable truth of their " 'twas to be." He agrees with Angel Clare's denomination of "It" as unsympathetic. He believes that even so fine a woman as Tess is of no more consequence than a fly before the universe, that she is caught like a "bird in a springe." No character, not even Alec, is truly responsible for his fate. When Angel has been cruelly intolerant of Tess, Hardy asks what this harshness is, compared to the "universal harshness out of which they grow; the harshness of the position towards the temperament, of the means towards the aims, of today towards yesterday, of hereafter towards today." But he never denominates this harshness as active or conscious. He does not even give It a name in the novel. He merely states, "So do flux and reflux—the rhythm of change—alternate and persist in everything under the sky." This rhythm of change, before which human beings must willy-nilly bow, operates as relentlessly as it has in earlier novels, in such a way that birth often seems something which may be palliated, never justified.

The "intolerable antilogy of making figments feel" is emphasized as it has not been since *The Return of the Native*. Consciousness is a veiled damnation, for it makes us realize our true situation. It has caused a "decline of belief in a beneficent Power," making melancholy chronic. The necessity of taking thought has made the heavens gray. More importantly, consciousness has made us aware of desires that cannot be satisfied. Even starving hopes persist; there is an "irresistible, universal, automatic tendency to find sweet pleasure somewhere," an "invincible instinct towards self-delight." But there is unfortunately another force which works against this instinct. At work everywhere is "the inherent will to enjoy, and the circumstantial will against enjoyment." Those characters who understand their situation feel with Tess, even in happy times, that all good fortune will be scourged out of them later in heaven's usual way. The gods are persistent ironists. By the time we learn, our experience has incapacitated us for doing. "In the ill-judged execution of a well-judged plan," "the call seldom produces the comer." Nature infrequently says "See" when the saying leads to happiness; It only allows clear vision when the body's hide-and-seek has become an outworn game. So, when Tess is ready for love, she meets Alec rather than Angel. So, when Angel learns how he has misjudged Tess, it is too late, and Angel and Tess can be happy together for only a short time, for the eternal flux and reflux dictate that their inherent will to enjoy be counterbalanced by the circumstantial will against enjoyment.

—Harvey Curtis Webster, *On a Darkling Plain: The Art and Thought of Thomas Hardy* (Chicago: University of Chicago Press, 1947), pp. 173–75

❖

[Dorothy Van Ghent (b. 1907) is the author of *Willa Cather* (1964), *Keats: The Myth of the Hero* (1983), and *The English Novel: Form and Function* (1953), from which the following extract is taken. Here, Van Ghent explores the symbolic use of the earth in *Tess*.]

In *Tess*, of all his novels, the earth is most actual as a dramatic factor—that is, as a factor of causation; and by this we refer simply to the long stretches of earth that have to be trudged in order that a person may get from one place to another, the slowness of the business, the irreducible reality of it (for one has only one's feet), its grimness of soul-wearing fatigue and shelterlessness and doubtful issue at the other end of the journey where nobody may be at home. One thinks, in immediate comparison, of Egdon Heath in *The Return of the Native*. Except for one instance—when Mrs. Yeobright has a far walk to Clym's cottage, and Clym, unforewarned, fails to meet her, and she turns away—the heath in *The Return* exists peripherally and gratuitously in relation to the action, on the one hand as the place where the action happens to happen (an action has to happen somewhere), and on the other, as a metaphor—a metaphorical reflection of the loneliness of human motive, of the inertia of unconscious life, of the mystery of the enfolding darkness; but it is not a dramatically causative agent and its particular quality is not *dramatically* necessary. In *The Mayor of Casterbridge,* the Roman ruins round about the town of Casterbridge are a rather more complicated metaphor, for they are works of man that have fallen into earth; they speak mutely of the anonymity of human effort in historical as well as in geological time; their presence suggests also the classic pattern of the Mayor's tragedy, the ancient repetitiveness of self-destruction; and they provide thus a kind of guarantee or confirming signature of the heroism of the doomed human enterprise. But the Mayor could have had his tragedy in a town with no Roman ruins about it at all; they are, even more than Egdon Heath, gratuitous, and their gratuitousness leads Hardy into some pedantry of documentation to support their metaphorical standing in the story. In *Tess* the earth is *primarily not a metaphor but a real thing* that one has to move on in order to get anywhere or do anything, and it constantly acts in its own motivating, causational substantiality by being there in the way of human purposes to encounter, to harass them, detour them, seduce them, defeat them.

In the accident of Prince's death, the road itself is, in a manner of speaking, responsible, merely by being the same road that the mail cart travels. The seduction of Tess is as closely related, causally, to the distance between Trantridge and Chaseborough as it is to Tess's naïveté and to Alec's egoism; the physical distance itself causes Tess's fatigue and provides Alec's opportunity. The insidiously demoralizing effect of Tess's desolate journeys on foot as she seeks dairy work and field work here and there after the collapse of her marriage, brutal months that are foreshortened to the plodding trip over the chalk uplands to Flintcomb-Ash, is, again, as directly as anything, an effect of the irreducible *thereness* of the territory she has to cover. There are other fatal elements in her ineffectual trip from the farm to Emminster to see Clare's parents, but fatal above all is the distance she must walk to see people who can have no foreknowledge of her coming and who are not at home when she gets there. Finally, with the uprooting and migration of the Durbeyfield family on Old Lady Day, the simple fatality of the earth as earth, in its measurelessness and anonymousness, with people having to move over it with no place to go, is decisive in the final event of Tess's tragedy—her return to Alec, for Alec provides at least a place to go.

The dramatic motivation provided by natural earth is central to every aspect of the book. It controls the style: page by page *Tess* has a wrought density of texture that is fairly unique in Hardy; symbolic depth is communicated by the physical surface of things with unhampered transparency while the homeliest conviction of fact is preserved ("The upper half of each turnip had been eaten off by the live-stock"); and one is aware of style not as a specifically verbal quality but as a quality of observation and intuition that are here—very often—wonderfully identical with each other, a quality of lucidity. Again, it is because of the *actual* motivational impact of the earth that Hardy is able to use setting and atmosphere for a symbolism that, considered in itself, is so astonishingly blunt and rudimentary. The green vale of Blackmoor, fertile, small, enclosed by hills, lying under a blue haze—the vale of birth, the cradle of innocence. The wide misty setting of Talbothays dairy, "oozing fatness and warm ferments," where the "rush of juices could almost be heard below the hiss of fertilization"—the sensual dream, the lost Paradise. The starved uplands of Flintcomb-Ash, with their ironic mimicry of the organs of generation, "myriads of loose white flints in bulbous, cusped, and phallic shapes," and the dun consuming ruin of the swede field—the mockery of impotence, the exile. Finally, that immensely courageous use of setting, Stonehenge and the stone of sacrifice. Obvious as these symbolisms are, their deep stress is maintained by Hardy's naturalistic premise. The earth exists here as Final Cause, and its omnipresence affords constantly to Hardy the textures that excited his eye and care, but affords them wholly charged with dramatic, causational necessity; and the symbolic values of setting are constituted, in large part, by the responses required of the characters themselves in their relationship with the earth.

> —Dorothy Van Ghent, "On *Tess of the D'Urbervilles*," *The English Novel: Form and Function* (New York: Holt, Rinehart & Winston, 1953), pp. 201–3

❖

ALLAN BRICK ON THE INFLUENCE OF MILTON ON *TESS OF THE D'URBERVILLES*

[Allan Brick is a professor of English at Hunter College of the City University of New York. In this extract, Brick probes the influence of Milton on *Tess,* showing how Angel and Tess are similar to the Adam and Eve of *Paradise Lost.*]

Tess beginning "Phase the Second (Maiden No More)" is a fallen being starting the first phase of real human life with the burden of original sin already upon her. She is Milton's Eve of Book X, judged by his Christ: "Thy sorrow I will greatly multiply / By thy conception; children thou shalt bring / In sorrow forth, and to thy husband's will / Thine shall submit, he over thee shall rule" (193–196). Having ended a period of cohabitation with Alec, she trudges homeward to Marlott, weary under a heavy basket and large bundle. She passes through Trantridge, a country "terribly beautiful to Tess to-day, for since her eyes last fell upon it she had learnt that the serpent hisses where the sweet birds sing . . . " She is "verily another girl." But after giving birth to the child, and being forced to bury it in unhallowed ground, she finds employment as a milkmaid in Blackmoor Vale, a fecund cow-laden land where immediately her hopes mingle "with the sunshine in an ideal photosphere" and she hears "a pleasant voice in every breeze." Taking up residence at Talbothays Dairy, she is prepared for "Phase the Third (The Rally)"—which is to be her true beginning in earth's illusory Eden.

Her Adam is Angel Clare, a young man who comes direct from the high gentility to which Tess—more earth-bound than he, and therefore more experienced in nature's ways—has aspired. Indeed, compared with Tess's, Angel's early training has been literally divine, administered to him by his Calvinist-clergyman father. Angel at Talbothays is Adam in a created but prelapsarian condition in which divine edicts seem to exist only as a code of morality cut off from the unseen and therefore unimaginable God who is said to have made them; he is the clergyman's son away from home. Angel should be characterized by Milton's definition for Adam: "He for God, she for God in him"; but he is not, for the vertical line is cut off, and, whereas Tess—certainly "for God in him"—fills the part of Eve here, he is simply for God in himself. He is an agnostic standing on an intellectual and moralistic system which, erected by himself, he believes absolutely sound. Rather than perceive humbly, tentatively, through light given to him, Angel imposes his oversimplifying, sentimentalist vision upon complex reality, easily believing the Talbothays Dairy is Eden and Tess his perfect Eve. Angel's self-conceived condition is that of William Dewy ("dewy" are the early Talbothays mornings in which Angel simulates Paradise with Tess), Farmer Crick's fabled character who, pursued by a bull, brought the beast to its knees by playing the " 'Tivity Hymn" even though it was not Christmas Eve. Hearing of William, Angel responds: "It's a curious story;

it carries us back to medieval times, when faith was a living thing." This comment marks Angel's introduction into the novel (though the story had been prompted by one of the male milkers calling to him, "You should get your harp, sir; not but what a fiddle is best," to which the addressee is reported to have responded "Why?"); and thus, with the identification clear, Farmer Crick's story serves as a cartoon for the way Angel would subdue animal reality by imposing his own divine vision upon it. Continuing his response, Angel says he has no doubt of the story's veracity, and "Tess's attention was thus attracted to the dairyman's interlocutor." "Thus" indeed is Tess revivified into Eden—lured back into believing in her maidenhood; from here on she becomes recreated Eve—victim again of the beliefs in her singular beauty and d'Urberville immortality—as she develops in response to Angel's enforced vision. Regenerated by the faith of Angel, sloughing off the torpor of an unreflecting union with nature, she will grow into being as a conscious individual, as subject and object of human love.

Tess's rebirth under Angel's magical perception is dramatized several pages later when she is paralleled with the bull of Farmer Crick's story. Walking in the garden on a summer evening when all the elements of nature seem miraculously alive, Tess is jolted out of a reverie by a "strumming of strings"—of course from Angel's harp. As the notes wander "in the still air with a stark quality like that of nudity," Tess, "like a fascinated bird, could not leave the spot." Drawn toward the performer, Tess "was conscious of neither time nor space. The exaltation which she had described as being producible at will by gazing at a star came now without any determination of hers; she undulated upon the thin notes of the second-hand harp, and their harmonies passed like breezes through her, bringing tears into her eyes." The price that Tess is forced to pay for her rebirth is the loss of her intimate relationship with nature. Interrupted by the strummings are ominous warnings from the trees which, as she tells Angel, "all seem very fierce and cruel and as if they said, 'I'm coming! Beware of me! Beware of me!' But *you*, sir, can raise up dreams with your music, and drive all such horrid fancies away!" Hearkening only to Angel, Tess is thrust tragically upward from her condition of oneness with nature and the folk; and his zeal to elevate and educate her ("Would you like to take up a course of study—history, for example?") develops her human tendency to be a skeptical philosopher. Her consequent accomplishment and pride in courageous discovery and assertion are as dooming as they are admirable.

—Allan Brick, "Paradise and Consciousness in Hardy's *Tess*," *Nineteenth-Century Fiction* 17, No 2 (September 1962): 121–23

❖

IRVING HOWE ON FEMALE SEXUALITY IN *TESS OF THE D'URBERVILLES*

[Irving Howe (1920–1993), for many years a professor of English at Hunter College of the City University of New York, was one of the most distinguished literary and social critics of our time. He is the author of many books, including *Literary Modernism* (1967), *William Faulkner: A Critical Study* (1975), and *Leon Trotsky* (1978). In this extract, Howe comments on Hardy's ability to understand female sexuality throughout his work and especially in *Tess*.]

Throughout Hardy's fiction, even in his lesser novels, there is a curious power of sexual insinuation, almost as if he were not locked into the limits of masculine perception but could shuttle between, or for moments yoke together, the responses of the two sexes. This gift for creeping intuitively into the emotional life of women Hardy shared with a contemporary, George Gissing, though he was quite free of that bitter egocentrism which marred Gissing's work. And at the deepest level of his imagination, Hardy held to a vision of the feminine that was thoroughly traditional in celebrating the maternal, the protective, the fecund, the tender, the life-giving. It was Hardy's openness to the feminine principle that drew D. H. Lawrence to his work and led him to see there, with some justice, a kinship with his own. One may speculate that precisely those psychological elements which led Hardy to be so indulgent toward male passivity also enabled him to be so receptive to feminine devices. He understood and could portray aggression; but at least as a writer, he did not allow it to dominate or corrode his feelings about the other sex—and that, incidentally, is one reason he does not care to pass judgment on his characters. The feminine admixture is very strong in his work, a source both of his sly humor and his profound sympathy.

It is in *Tess of the D'Urbervilles* that this side of Hardy comes through with the most striking vitality. The book stands at the center of Hardy's achievement, if not as his greatest then certainly his most characteristic, and those readers or critics who cannot accept its emotional ripeness must admit that for them Hardy is not a significant novelist. For in *Tess* he stakes everything on his sensuous apprehension of a young woman's life, a girl who is at once a simple milkmaid and an archetype of feminine strength. Nothing finally matters in the novel nearly so much as Tess herself: not the other characters, not the philosophic underlay, not the social setting. In her violation, neglect and endurance, Tess comes to seem Hardy's most radical claim for the redemptive power of suffering; she stands, both in the economy of the book and as a figure rising beyond its pages and into common memory, for the unconditional authority of feeling.

Tess is one of the greatest examples we have in English literature of how a writer can take hold of a cultural stereotype and, through the sheer intensity of his affection, pare and purify it into something that is morally ennobling. Tess derives from Hardy's involvement with and reaction against the Victorian cult of chastity, which from the beginning of his career he had known to be corrupted by meanness and hysteria. She falls. She violates the standards and conventions of her day. And yet, in her incomparable vibrancy and lovingness, she comes to represent a spiritualized transcendence of chastity. She dies three times, to live again:—first with Alec D'Urberville, then with Angel Clare, and lastly with Alec again. Absolute victim of her wretched circumstances, she is ultimately beyond their stain. She embodies a feeling for the inviolability of the person, as it brings the absolute of chastity nearer to the warming Christian virtue of charity. Through a dialectic of negation, Tess reaches purity of spirit even as she fails to satisfy the standards of the world.

Perhaps because she fails to satisfy them? Not quite. What we have here is not the spiritual sensationalism of the Dostoevsky who now and again indulges himself in the notion that a surrender to licentiousness is a necessary condition for spiritual rebirth. Hardy's view is a more innocent one, both purer and less worldly. He does not seek the abyss nor glory in finding it. He is not a phenomenologist of the perverse. But as a man deeply schooled in the sheer difficulty of life, he does recognize that there is a morality of being as well as of doing, an imperative to compassion which weakens the grip of judgment. Once educated to humility, we do not care to judge Tess at all: we no longer feel ourselves qualified. And that, I think, is a triumph of the moral imagination.

In staking out these claims for *Tess of the D'Urbervilles* I recognize that Hardy's vision of Tess can hardly satisfy the rigorous morality of Protestantism which was a part of his heritage. Other forces are at work, both pre- and post-Christian: the stoicism of the folk ballad, from whose wronged heroines Tess descends, and the moral experiment of romanticism. Hardy could no more avoid the conditioning influence of romanticism than a serious writer can now avoid that of modernism; it was part of the air he breathed. His romanticism enabled Hardy to break past the repressions of the Protestant ethic and move into a kindlier climate shared by Christian charity and pagan acceptance; but it was also romanticism, with its problematic and perverse innovations, which threatened his wish for a return to a simple, primitive Christianity. In *Tess of the D'Urbervilles* the romantic element appears most valuably as an insistence upon the right of the individual person to create the terms of his being, despite the pressures and constraints of the external world. Yet, because Tess is a warmhearted and unpretentious country girl barely troubled by intellectual ambition, Hardy's stress is upon the right of the person and not, as it will be in *Jude the Obscure,* upon the subjective demands of personality. Sue Bridehead anticipates the modern cult of personality in all its urgency and clamor; Tess Durbeyfield represents something more deeply rooted in the substance of instinctual life.

—Irving Howe, *Thomas Hardy* (New York: Macmillan, 1967), pp. 109–11

❖

BERT G. HORNBACK ON THE STONEHENGE SCENE IN *TESS OF THE D'URBERVILLES*

[Bert G. Hornback (b. 1935) is a professor of English at the University of Notre Dame and the author of several books, including *"The Hero of My Life": Essays on Dickens* (1981) and studies of Dickens's *Great Expectations* (1987) and George Eliot's *Middlemarch* (1988). In this extract from his book on Hardy, Hornback analyzes the Stonehenge scene in *Tess,* finding it the central scene in the novel in its metaphoric and symbolic significance.]

The scene at Stonehenge is the most important in the novel. Hardy concentrates his whole effort here to insist on the size of his heroine and the greatness of her tragedy. At the same time this scene is the final and climactic representation of Hardy's own nondramatic point of view, and the voice of the critic speaks, proclaiming Tess the "victim."

There are two major sets of metaphors at work in this scene which finally come together as one in the murder of Alec. The first is the metaphor of blood, suggesting both Tess's loss of her virginity and her final destruction. Tess wears a red ribbon at the traditional May-walk—and she is "the only one of the white company who could boast of such a pronounced adornment." She is splashed with the blood of the dying Prince, after he is speared by the shaft of the mail cart. As a result of this misfortunate loss of the horse, Tess allows herself to be persuaded to visit her "relatives" at Trantridge. There she is fed the ripe, red strawberries from Alec's garden, and is decked in a spectacle of red roses, and pricks her chin on the thorns. After her seduction, she meets the sign painter who accuses her in "staring vermillion words." She returns to Marlott, and while working in the field her arm is bruised and abraided by the stubble, and bleeds. Then, life and convention having pursued her like fates or furies, and her crime having become so complex as to allow no easy retribution or resolution, Tess kills Alec, and his blood stains—crudely—through the ceiling as an ace of hearts. Though Tess's blood is not actually shed in the end, she is sacrificed symbolically at the place which supposedly would have required, in its own time, the spilling of blood.

MATIGNON HIGH SCHOOL LIBRARY
1 MATIGNON ROAD
CAMBRIDGE, MASS. 02140

The second pattern of symbolic reference used to prepare for the Stonehenge scene is a series of three white coffins or altars. The first is the "empty stone coffin" in the churchyard of the old d'Urberville mansion, in which Angel places Tess on the night of their marriage and mutual confession. Her past forces her, symbolically and in actuality, toward her future at Stonehenge, and disallows any free and satisfactory existence between those times. Tess has only three experiences in life: her seduction, and the twin acts of her revenge or expiation and her sacrifice. Her other experience, falling in love with Angel and marrying him, is denied to her in the meaning of his sleepwalk to the open coffin with her in his arms, and in her second burial on the altar at Stonehenge. The second of the stone symbols appears in Chapter 52, as the Durbeyfields arrive at Kingsbere and Tess enters the church of her ancestors. She passes "near an altar-tomb, the oldest of them all, on which was a recumbent figure." The figure is not an effigy, however; it is Alec. The stone slab on which he lies prefigures, ironically, the bed in which he is murdered. That bed, its white sheets stained with his blood, is the last of the stone symbols and the one in which the altar-coffin and blood metaphors are united. It is the altar of Tess's act of expiation for her fault. Although she finally does "annihilate" her past by destroying Alec, she does not really escape it, nor does she gain a future, except in her brief, wild honeymoon with Angel and in the lives of Angel and 'Liza-Lu beyond the end of the novel.

Tess's existence is governed by the law of tragedy relentlessly imposed and enforced. Hardy's insistence on his theme insures this. Though Tess is seduced, she is still—or finally—a pure woman. Her purity is redeemed throughout the novel in her heroism, and she is fulfilled in the end. The fulfillment is tragic, however, and thus in some sense it is sacrifice as well. It would be easy to say that Tess is sacrificed to the conventions of man's limitations, which is what Hardy wants to say, in part. More significant, however, is Tess's sacrifice of herself for the sake of her honesty and dignity; and in this Tess redeems man from his limitations, and achieves her freedom.

Though the scene at Stonehenge is not the best accomplishment of Hardy's art, it is his most ambitious attempt at rendering the world of the action in metaphoric and symbolic terms.

With Stonehenge, he suddenly expands the dimensions and significance of Tess's tragedy to the extremes of suggestive reference. Tess is made to belong to Stonehenge, to its immensity in time and its incomprehensible towering aspect. The scene, however, may be too large for the rest of the novel, despite the preparation for it in the suggestions of sacrifice discussed above. Tess's tragic size is to be discovered primarily in the representative aspect of her life, as this is suggested by the history of the ancient line of d'Urbervilles, and the intensity of her existence is represented in the coincidental intrusions and recurrences of the past in the present. But nothing quite like Stonehenge can be anticipated from this. Stonehenge could have fit in *The Return of the Native* easily enough, and perhaps the texture of *The Mayor of Casterbridge* would have been enriched by the addition of another stage to go with Maumbury Ring and Mai-Dun. But in a novel not set physically on timeless, eternal Egdon Heath or amid Roman and prehistoric ruins, Stonehenge seems perhaps too expansive and too much a symbolic place.

But these are aesthetic considerations. And though it may be argued that the Stonehenge scene is symbolically awkward or aesthetically outsized, this does not diminish its thematic and philosophic significance. Angel tells Tess that Stonehenge is "older than the centuries; older than the d'Urbervilles." And that it is so is just the point. Tess's tragedy has been suggested as the general tragedy of man, heightened and intensified by the conventional intrusion of the past—and its fault—into the present. This recurrence of the past has been supported, metaphorically, through the use of Tess's ancestry. Suddenly, now, the d'Urberville history is not enough; Tess's life and fate are greater and more significant than the d'Urberville history can indicate. As Tess becomes conscious of her relation to Stonehenge, we are asked to accept on the strength of this new metaphor of setting a greater symbolic dimension for the whole novel. Stonehenge is the old "heathen temple" where sacrifices were made to the sun in primal days, before the worship of any modern God. Tess is placed on the altar stone of that ancient worship, and Hardy remarks at the close that "the President of the Immortals, in Aeschylean phrase, had ended his sport with Tess." This would make it seem that Tess is sacrificed to the gods, to Fate, to the unsympathetic manipulator of man's destiny. Yet Tess's fault is her own volitional tragic fault, not an imposition of a necessary fate upon her from the beginning. Her fate is determined, in the tradition of tragedy, by her own act—by the act that initiates the action of the rest of the tragedy. And though her final destruction at Wintoncester is accomplished at the hands of men acting from the straight, cruel standards of society, it is done with Tess's full and understanding submission.

—Bert G. Hornback, *The Metaphor of Chance: Vision and Technique in the Works of Thomas Hardy* (Athens: Ohio University Press, 1971), pp. 119–21

❖

JOHN BAYLEY ON TESS'S TRANSFORMATION

[John Bayley (b. 1925) is a distinguished British critic of English and Russian literature. Among his many works are *The Romantic Survival* (1957), *The Characters of Love* (1960), *Shakespeare and Tragedy* (1981), and *Housman's Poems* (1992). In this extract from *An Essay on Hardy* (1978), Bayley examines the changes Tess undergoes throughout the novel, as seen by Angel and the reader.]

In terms of form, then, Tess is a triumph of *non-realisation,* and it is this which makes her so totally different from the earlier heroines, even though, in successive detail, she is composed of the same elements as they are. The climax of the triumph, which vindicates this idea of form at the same time as it strikes the decisive blow in the plot, is Angel's discovery that she is not the same person as the one he has been infatuated with. He is, of course, absolutely right. And the manner in which he sustains the blow subtly underwrites the nature of Tess as a changed, or rather as a specifically indeterminate, being. For it emphasises in the most physical way possible his own continuity, in an ordinary humdrum way, and as the character we know:

Clare performed the irrelevant act of stirring the fire; the intelligence has not even yet got to the bottom of him. After stirring the embers he rose to his feet; all the force of her disclosure had imparted itself now. His face had withered. In the strenuousness of his concentration he treadled fitfully on the floor. He could not, by any contrivance, think closely enough; that was the meaning of his vague movement. When he spoke it was in the most inadequate, commonplace voice of the many varied tones she had heard from him.

Clare's consciousness is seen as a progress which has now become as laborious and impeded as possible, but which is none the less bound to go on. That inadequate commonplace voice which is unfamiliar to Tess is quite natural to the reader, for it suggests both the plodding of ordinary sequent consciousness and the weaknesses in Clare which the reader, but not Tess, is already well aware of. 'He tried desperately to advance among the new conditions in which he stood', and his impulse is to get up and walk. *Clare is experiencing as a personal drama the sense of Tess which for the reader is a sense of the book's form;* and conversely she is brought up against the limitations which make him, beside her, a very ordinary sort of literary conception.

He sees her discontinuity as something almost repellent— 'her cheek was flaccid, and her mouth had almost the aspect of a little round hole'—and in the physical oppression of the scene the magical Tess, the 'visionary essence of woman' who produced a love 'imaginative and ethereal', and in Clare 'a fastidious emotion which could jealously guard the loved one against his very self'—all are reduced to sorry actuality; and Tess herself to a pathos of the commonplace which seems connected less with her confession than with the general nature of disillusionment:

> 'O Tess, forgiveness does not apply to the case! You were one person; now you are another. My God—how can forgiveness meet such a grotesque—prestidigitation as that!'
> He paused, contemplating this definition;

Becoming aware of the change in her own image she gives way to a self-pity all the more pathetic for being so commonplace. It is typical of Hardy to have so involved himself and us in Tess's discontinuity that we do not dissociate ourselves from

Clare's separation from her: the form involves us in it. Moreover the tendency of the scene is to emphasise with a greater realism than at any time before how necessarily primitive Tess is, as simple and elementary a human being as Marian or Retty Priddle, from whom the previous vision of Hardy, as of Angel Clare, effortlessly separated her. At that time she *was* different; now her being seems as crude in its animal vulnerability as theirs.

In this again there is nothing as theoretical as Hardy's thesis that the milkmaid and the *grande dame* are the same in basic instinct and behaviour. He makes, indeed, an artifice out of something quite different: that she can have the tone of either from moment to moment. A striking instance is after the demise of the baby Sorrow, when she asks the parson to give him Christian burial, as if he had been properly baptised; and with 'the natural feelings of a tradesman' whose customers are botching the job themselves, he is disposed to say her own performance of the rite means nothing, but then, relenting, finds himself trapped in Tess's logic. Her query—'another matter—why?'—has the imperiousness of the lady of the manor, but there is an immediate acoustic return to the note of the haggler's daughter when she bursts out with 'I'll never come to your church no more'.

Tess is not the first of Hardy's characters to slip inconspicuously between one kind of social stance and another, a process very different from Dickens's frankly fairy-tale convention in the matter, and made possible by the sober accuracy with which Hardy—from personal observation—can enter on the inside at several social levels, whereas both Dickens and Meredith clung to their status as fairy princes who had entered into their rightful inheritance among the gentry. Hardy's note in the *Life* on the pleasure of watching, in a grand London drawing-room, the tea poured out by the gentle and kindly Winifred Herbert, who used to tell him about her forthcoming marriage—always referring to her fiancé as 'he'—and who wondered if he would give her name to one of his characters, shows the kind of metamorphosis that took place in his imagination of Tess. To find so sympathetic and unassuming a person in this aristocratic family must have been as enchanting an experience for Hardy as it was for Angel Clare to find a Tess among the milkmaids.

Tess's confession to Clare is an acute form of the disillusion that follows enchantment. Tess as wife would in any case be due for the reaction that marriage always brings in Hardy; and stripped of her other quasi-aristocratic persona she becomes all peasant, wearisome precisely in the degree that she is dumb and pitiful. Years later Hardy answered a query about Tess— admittedly with a touch of that exasperation such intrusions always aroused in him—by saying that of course Clare would quickly have tired of her, because the disparity between them, in terms of class and outlook, was too great. There is more than a hint of this in the novel itself, for misfortune in Hardy, like the sudden death of the young heiress in *An Indiscretion,* is often a symptom of—or a substitute for—the less visible unsuitability which weighs life down, but can have no place in the conventions of melodrama.

—John Bayley, *An Essay on Hardy* (Cambridge: Cambridge University Press, 1978), pp. 170–73

❖

PENNY BOUMELHA ON TESS'S SEXUALITY

[Penny Boumelha is Jury Professor of English Language and Literature at the University of Adelaide in Australia. She has written *Charlotte Brontë* (1990) and *Thomas Hardy and Women* (1982), from which the following extract is taken. Here, Boumelha argues that Tess is doomed both by her sexuality and by her lack of calculation.]

Tess of the d'Urbervilles, as one contemporary reviewer remarked, is 'peculiarly the Woman's Tragedy'. If Tess can be said to have a tragic 'flaw', it is her sexuality, which is, in this novel, her 'nature' as a woman. Her sexuality is above all provocative: she is a temptress to the convert Alec, an Eve to Angel Clare. Such are her sexual attractions that she is obliged to travesty herself into ' "a mommet of a maid" ' in order to protect herself from 'aggressive admiration.' Her sexuality is constructed above all through the erotic response of the narrator, and it was surely this that gave rise to Mowbray Morris' sneering objections:

> Poor Tess's sensual qualifications for the part of heroine are paraded over and over again with a persistence like that of a horse-dealer egging on some wavering customer to a deal, or a slave-dealer appraising his wares to some full-blooded pasha.

Morris had evidently not realised how far he is implicating himself, as a male reader, in that image of the 'wavering customer'. It is interesting to note, by the way, that Edmund Gosse drew a clear distinction between the responses of male and female readers to the novel; he contrasted the 'ape-leading and shrivelled spinster' who had reviewed *Tess* for the *Saturday Review* with the 'serious male public' who apprecated its qualities.

Set against this provocative sexual quality is a lack of calculation, essential if Tess is not to become a posing and self-dramatising *femme fatale* in the style of Felice Charmond. She never declares herself as either virginal or sexually available, and yet her experience is bounded by the power that both these images exercise. Hardy tries to preserve a narrow balance between her awareness of this sexual force (for if she remains wholly unaware, she is merely a passive and stupid victim) and her refusal deliberately to exploit it (for that would involve her too actively as a temptress). The problem becomes acute at the point of her break from Angel:

> Tess's feminine hope—shall we confess it—had been so obstinately recuperative as to revive in her surreptitious visions of a domiciliary intimacy continued long enough to break down his coldness even against his judgment. Though unsophisticated in the usual sense, she was not incomplete; and it would have denoted deficiency of womanhood if she had not instinctively known what an argument lies in propinquity. Nothing else would serve her, she knew, if this failed. It was wrong to hope in what was of the nature of strategy, she said to herself: yet that sort of hope she could not extinguish.

The archness of that parenthetical 'shall we confess it' and the elaborately distancing abstract and Latinate vocabulary testify to the difficulty of negotiating this area of a consciousness that must not become too conscious. The shared pronoun ('shall *we* confess it') hovers awkwardly between implying a suddenly female narrator and pulling the implied male reader into a conspiratorial secret (woman and their little ways) that remains concealed from Tess. He is obliged to fall back on the old standby of instinct (and, on the next page, intuition) for an explanation of a knowledge that Tess must have, in order not to be deficient in womanhood, and must not have, in order to avoid falling into anything 'of the nature of strategy'. 'Purity' is, in a sense, enforced upon Tess by the difficulty of representing for her a self-aware mode of sexuality.

For Tess is doomed by her sexuality in a quite different way from Felice Charmond or Eustacia Vye. She does not share their urgency of desire to be desired, nor their restless dissatisfaction with the actual relationships in which that desire is partially satisfied. Both of those women are complicit in the circumscribing of their identity by their sexuality, and of their experience by their relationships with men. Tess, on the other hand, is trapped by a sexuality which seems at times almost irrelevant to her own experience and sense of her own identity. She is doomed by her 'exceptional physical nature' and by the inevitability of an erotic response from men. That response binds her to male images and fantasies: to the pink cheeks and rustic innocence of Angel's patronising pastoralism, and to the proud indifference that Alec finds so piquantly challenging. Her sexuality, provocative without intent, seems inherently guilty by virtue of the reactions it arouses in others: 'And there was revived in her the wretched sentiment which had often come to her before, that in inhabiting the fleshly tabernacle with which Nature had endowed her she was somehow doing wrong.' 'Liza-Lu, the 'spiritualized image of Tess,' is spiritualised by the execution of Tess, expunging the wrong-doing and expiating the guilt of her woman's sexuality. 'Liza-Lu and Angel Clare give an openly fantasy ending to the novel, in a de-eroticized relationship that nevertheless contravenes socially constituted moral law far more clearly than any of Tess's, since a man's marriage with his sister-in-law remained not only illegal but also tainted with the stigma of incest until the passing of the controversial Deceased Wife's Sister Act (after several previous failed attempts), in 1907. The echo of *Paradise Lost* in the last sentence of *Tess* has often been remarked, but it is notable that the novel in fact offers a curiously inverted image of Milton's fallen world. The post-lapsarian world of *Tess* is attenuated ('Liza-Lu is only 'half girl, half woman,' and both she and Clare seem to have 'shrunk' facially) by expulsion from sexuality, and not by the loss of a pre-sexual innocence. In Tess are imaged both a Paradise of sexuality (abundant, fecund, succulent) and the guilt of knowledge that inheres within it.

> —Penny Boumelha, *Thomas Hardy and Women: Sexual Ideology and Narrative Form* (Brighton, UK: Harvester Press, 1982), pp. 123–26

❖

Bruce Johnson on Hardy and Darwin

[Bruce Johnson (b. 1933), a professor of English at American International College (Springfield, Massachusetts), is the author of *Conrad's Models of Mind* (1971) and *True Correspondence* (1983), a book on Hardy from which the following extract is taken. Here, Johnson traces the possible influence of Charles Darwin's theory of evolution on *Tess*.]

It would appear, then, that one of the keys to understanding Tess lies precisely in Hardy's understanding of this crucial late-Victorian view of the relation between past and present. We begin, I think, to appreciate its full flavor by realizing that there are even implications for historiography in these early anthropologists—especially in ⟨Sir James George⟩ Frazer and ⟨Edward Burnett⟩ Tylor. Henceforth it will be very difficult for historians to write without borrowing some late-Victorian evolutionary ideas about culture, ideas that come mainly from the evolutionary anthropologists.

For Hardy, it is obviously Darwin who is crucial in these matters. Yet the details of Hardy's vivid reaction to Darwin have been largely a mystery for generations of critics. That Hardy emphasized the evolutionary connections among all life (the relatedness of man and "lower" forms) above the infamous "survival of the fittest" is a point insufficiently emphasized by those who discuss him. It was made some fifteen years ago in an article by Elliot B. Gose, Jr. Gose quotes the crucial passage from Hardy's notebook: "The discovery of the law of evolution which revealed that all organic creations are of one family, shifted the center of altruism from humanity to the whole conscious world collectively." Equally important is Hardy's note written before he began *Tess:* "Altruism, or the Golden Rule, or whatever 'Love your Neighbor as Yourself' may be called, will ultimately be brought about I think by the pain we see in others reacting on ourselves, as if we and they were a part of one body. Mankind, in fact, may be and possibly will be viewed as members of one corporeal frame." Whether Comte or Schopenhauer is more nearly reflected here, the evolutionary bias is toward creative evolution, and toward seeing Darwin's impact less in Spencerian terms than as integrating man with man and man with all life in some creative thrust. (One wonders about the amount of biology even in Schopenhauer's avowedly "metaphysical" argument for the noumenal unity of man, the problem of seeing personality as "maya" to be penetrated by the initiate.) All critics see "creative evolution" in *The Dynasts,* with its conception of blind Will gradually becoming conscious, but no one other than Gose has, to my knowledge, seen the importance of this emphasis in Hardy's *entire* reaction to Darwin, early and late.

Gose sees Tess as the failure of "psychic evolution" toward some ultimate form of altruism for all living creatures, a failure confirmed by her murder of Alec. I need not summarize his article here, though it is the only place in Hardy criticism where the impact of Darwin and the comparative and evolutionary anthropologists (particularly Tylor in *Primitive Culture,* 1871, and Frazer in his early *Totemism,* 1887) is vividly imagined. To put the matter with what little simplicity it allows, Hardy was much given to thinking about evolution in its creative aspect and to speculating in fictive ways about the modification of natural evolutionary laws by man's self-conscious grasp of them and by ethical qualities emerging as "variations." Most of the Spencerian social analysis according to evolutionary principles was foreign to Hardy, who apparently took to heart Darwin's admonition that "In social animals it [natural selection] will adapt the structure of each individual for the benefit of the community." Still, Hardy's emphasis on the kinship of all creatures in an evolutionary way rather than on the ruthless struggle for existence [the Schopenhauerian Will surely resembles some aspects of this struggle] did not simply produce in him a straightforward desire to imagine characters in whom this "psychic evolution" toward some ultimate altruism could take place. If Tess's killing the wounded birds is evidence of some such capacity in her, it also suggests some of the dark implications of our aboriginal kinship with all life. The self-reflective, self-conscious mind of man is apparently necessary to sense this evolutionary kinship—yet it may be precisely this capacity that definitively separates us from other forms of life.

I depart from Elliot Gose when he uses his splendid sense of Hardy's involvement with the comparative and evolutionary anthropologists to call Tess a failed psychic evolution. It is no exaggeration to say that Hardy brooded fictively on the dramatic essence of the "struggle for existence" and—Spencer's phrase before it was Darwin's—the "survival of the fittest." Darwin seems to have been as much aware of and concerned about the metaphoric nature of that word "struggle" as Stanley Edgar Hyman was in his comments on *The Origin of Species*. The usually quiet drift toward existence or death on the "tangled bank" occasionally becomes, in Hardy, literally a tragic struggle of some kind of intrinsically natural man or woman to survive in a world where society has confusingly changed the less ambiguous rules of survival in nature. Thus in Tess we see her real affinities with basic natural processes, her limited but important participation in an ancient form of folk culture, her introduction to the byways and perversions of "modern" society, especially as Alec manifests them (and as they are symbolically rendered in connection with Alec and the modern threshing machine in that famous scene), and finally her betrayal by an imagined denial of modern society in Angel's Hellenic nature worship. Significantly, it is really only Angel's denial of any truly Darwinian knowledge of Nature that brings Tess down. Hardy imaginatively and systematically scrutinizes the idea of survival and indeed the whole question of who is fittest among human beings by subjecting Tess to, as it were, degrees of societal complication and changes in the quality and texture of societal complication. Angel's antisocietal idealism, it seems to me, is finally revealed as the most potent corruption of society.

—Bruce Johnson, *True Correspondence: A Phenomenology of Thomas Hardy's Novels* (Tallahassee: Florida State University Press, 1983), pp. 114–17

❖

Kristin Brady on Hardy's Treatment of Sexuality

[Kristin Brady (b. 1949) is a professor of English at the University of Western Ontario in Canada and the author of *The Short Stories of Thomas Hardy* (1982). In this extract, Brady examines the narrator's point of view in regard to Tess's sexuality.]

One can never ignore altogether the serious restrictions on Hardy as he attempted to treat female sexuality in *Tess*, but it would also be simplistic to attribute all the novel's ambivalence to Mrs Grundy. Much recent feminist criticism dwells on the extent to which Hardy's narrator seems himself to exhibit a fundamental ambivalence toward Tess's sexuality. The narrator's undeniably erotic fascination with her takes the form of a visual preoccupation with her physical presence, and it has even been suggested that the narrator derives an almost sadistic pleasure from Tess's suffering, that he shares in part the distorted views of her held by both Alec and Angel, and that he in some sense does himself violate her with his male voice and male eye. By the same token, the narrator seems to retreat from and close his eyes to the most explicit and direct manifestations of the sexuality which so fascinates him. As Penny Boumelha has perceptively remarked, Tess's sexuality is ultimately 'unknowable' and 'unrepresentable' by the narrator, and he withdraws completely from her consciousness at the most crucial points in her life: the moment when she was wakened to Alec's return in The Chase, the weeks following that scene when she was his mistress, the time of the discovery of her pregnancy and the birth of her child, the points when she decided to return to Alec and then to murder him and flee with

Angel. Major events often take place between chapters and phases of the book, and are conveyed to the reader only by the narrator's factual reference to their having happened. Indeed, Tess's real thoughts and feelings are rarely presented in the novel, except when she suffers the consequences of her actions. Her moral choices seem obscured in ambivalence, while their results are vividly and dramatically portrayed. The effect of these constant jumps in the narration is that the reader can have a firm sense of Tess's suffering and her role as victim, but a somewhat confused sense of her own participation in her fate. The issue of 'purity' is of course crucial here: if Tess's relationship with Alec was based in any sense on her own sexual desire, regardless of whether she 'loved' him or not, then she is not 'pure' in the rigid Victorian sense of that word; if, on the other hand, Tess was simply the passive victim of Alec's sexual aggression, then the question of her own sexuality becomes insignificant. Tess would then be simply a victim of circumstances, not a woman with complex feelings and responses.

Whether it was from external or internal pressures, Hardy obviously felt he had to walk a tightrope between these two conceptions of Tess. She is both the betrayed maid and the fallen woman, both the scapegoat and the tragic heroine complicitous in her own downfall. The repeated references in the novel to the Persephone myth and to *Paradise Lost* draw together her two roles: raped daughter of Nature sacrificed to the powers of the underworld, and tempted daughter of Nature punished for her act of pride.

While this contradictory portrait can be seen in part as a function of Hardy's own ambivalence about Tess, the results are not entirely negative ones. For although Hardy's portrayal of her never met his intended conception, the book still constitutes a considerable achievement in presenting the conflicting sensations and emotions that can be part of a sexual response. Hardy's own difficulties may, in fact, have contributed to the book's complexity, which lies in the way in which many of Tess's sexual feelings are buried deep within the texture of the narrative. What the novel lost in frankness after Hardy began to revise it may still be found in its rich ambivalences. In his handling of the scenes leading up to Tess's loss of virginity, for example, Hardy is extraordinarily subtle in depicting the sorts of sexual titillation that can be excited by a veteran seducer, especially in a woman like Tess, who has no knowledge or experience of sex. She is temporarily attracted to Alec even as she distrusts him and finds him repellent, and it is this bewildering combination of sensations and emotions that Hardy manages to convey to his Victorian audience.

The central ambivalence in *Tess of the d'Urbervilles* is of course the scene in The Chase, in which the narrator launches into polemics immediately after the description of Alec's discovery of Tess in a sound sleep. The story then leaps into the second phase in the novel, 'Maiden No More'—as if Tess's loss of virginity had taken place on the bare page between the two phases. From the time of the book's publication, the question of whether Tess was raped or seduced has divided critics, and the debate has still not been resolved with perfect clarity. Grindle and Gatrell's 'General Introduction' to the scholarly edition of the novel, for example, uses the words 'rape' and 'seduction' interchangeably, and G. Glen Wickens's fine essay on the Persephone myth speaks of the 'ambiguous moment' when seduction turns into rape. An aspect of the confusion, needless to say, lies not just in Hardy's novel but in the inadequacy of the words themselves. 'Rape' suggests physical force alone, while 'seduction' implies merely the pressure of enticement, and neither of the terms comes close to representing precisely how Alec d'Urberville awakened and then exploited the sexual instincts of Tess Durbeyfield. His most effective pressure, for example—both in The Chase and before her second submission to him at the end of the novel—lies in his appeals to her guilt about her responsibilities to her family. By helping them and so requiring gratitude of her, he makes Tess feel all the more compromised in her rebuffs of his sexual advances. If he did exert physical force on her in The Chase, that would have been just one form of his assault on her person.
    —Kristin Brady, "Tess and Alec: Rape or Seduction?," *Thomas Hardy Annual* No. 4 (1986): 129–31

❖

[Pamela L. Jekel (b. 1948) has written *Perfect Crime and How to Commit It* (1980) and *Thomas Hardy: A Chorus of Priorities* (1986), from which the following extract is taken. Here, Jekel outlines the "simple and allegorical" plot of *Tess*.]

The plot of *Tess* is simple and almost allegorical. It might have sprung from an old folk ballad or a legend from the country of which Hardy wrote. It concerns the "eternal triangle," the wronged woman who cannot escape her past sins, and the double standard of morality and purgation that such sin demanded in the Victorian era. In fact, Jean R. Brooks notes the existence of just such a ballad with a heroine called Patient Griselda—a high-born lady in disguise who becomes a milk-maid, is seduced by an aristocrat, murders her seducer, and finally hangs on the gallows for her crimes. Hardy, however, poses an additional challenge. He creates a powerful sympathy and reader identification with Tess and her situation and thereby questions social morality and her fate at the hands of that morality. In doing so, Hardy turns allegory to social polemic.

P. N. Furbank says that "*Tess* as a whole is a very different novel from its predecessors primarily because of its allegorical qualities." I would argue that *Tess* is a *better* novel in that it more closely intertwines Hardy's thought and art, but is not necessarily different from *The Woodlanders* or *The Return of the Native*, both allegorical in tone. With *Tess*, Hardy is at once more blatantly poetic and subtly more opinionated—in short, more himself—than he was either capable of or free to be in previous works. In *Tess*, we see passages like:

> Those [cows] that were spotted with white reflected the sun-shine in dazzling brilliancy, and the polished brass knobs on their horns glittered with something of military display. Their large-veined udders hung ponderous as sandbags, the teats sticking out like the legs of a gipsy's crock; and as each animal lingered for her turn to arrive the milk oozed forth and fell in drops to the ground.

Here is a rural poet revealed. We might expect Emma to dis-like *Tess*, in fact, for having "too much of cows in it."

Tess's story is extremely sombre to be sure, but it is a story with much grace and power. In spite of her hardships, Tess weaves a continuous thread of optimism and fortitude throughout the novel which becomes Hardy's hymn to the human spirit. Tess has an "invincible instinct towards self-delight" and an "automatic tendency to find sweet pleasure somewhere, which pervades all life." Her spirit of hopeful exuberance sustains her through what would be, without her, a melancholy life view indeed.

We see her sense of life (and Hardy's) in her relationship with the Clares. She knows she needs Angel not as a moralist but as a man. The elder Mr. Clare is shown by Hardy to be a sincere if narrow pietist who quotes from Corinthians I, "We are made as the filth of the world." "His creed," Hardy says, "quite amounted, on its negative side, to a renunciative philosophy which had cousinship with that of Schopenhauer and Leopardi." Like the old sign-painter who was putting up anti-sexual messages on walls, a painter who said he had been inspired by Mr. Clare, Hardy shows us "the last grotesque phase of a creed which had served mankind well in its time." Here is Hardy unconsciously gazing at one of his selves—his pessimism—and denouncing it with another—his humanism. And Tess, his handmaiden, says, "Pooh—I don't believe God said such things."

The simple plot of *Tess* is perhaps a clue to the meaning of the novel itself. Its similarity to a ballad makes it an expanded allegory of fate and self-determination. Hardy's subtitle informs the reader that Tess, "A Pure Woman," is a symbol; yet she becomes much more than a symbol. In her actions, she removes herself from traditional morality and social regulation and thus reestablishes an ancient, pagan, and somehow more modern morality and rationale for behavior. As Albert J. LaValley indicates:

> Hardy's novel, then, uses simplicity of plotting for complex purposes . . . to suggest the dual movement of pain and pleasure which Hardy saw as the movement of life itself.

Tess's plot, too, seems more carefully wrought than previous attempts. Early clues, forebodings, and premonitions subtly prepare the reader for later action. As early as Chapter Four, we hear an "elderly boozer" warn Joan Durbeyfield, "mind Tess don't get green malt on floor"—a rustic vernacular for getting pregnant which hardy slips past the censor. Also, his careful plotting of Tess's movements from Marlott to Trantridge, back to Marlott, on to Talbothays, to Flintcomb-Ash, Kingsbere, to Sandbourne, to Stonehenge, and finally to Wintonchester illustrates the tapestry of actions and locale he wove.

Tess of the d'Urbervilles is built of distinct and personal Hardy values. For the most part, Tess's views are close to Hardy's own. His indictment of the prevailing view of women as sexual objects, of the deceit often used in marriage, of the destructiveness and lure of passion, and of the overestimation of virginity are all echoed by Tess's refusal to accept such terms. For example, one important quality in Tess's character that influences her fate is her wholehearted devotion to the man she loves. Hardy stresses the essence of goodness that such devotion implies. He creates a heroine who often puts her man's welfare above her own, occasionally to her own detriment.

—Pamela L. Jekel, Thomas Hardy's Heroines: A Chorus of Priorities (Troy, NY: Whitston Publishing Co., 1986), pp. 158–60

❖

PETER J. CASAGRANDE ON ANGEL CLARE AND BEAUTY

[Peter J. Casagrande is a professor of English at the University of Kansas. Among his books are *Unity in Hardy's Novels* (1982) and *Hardy's Influence on the Modern Novel* (1987). In this extract from his study of *Tess* (1992), Casagrande explores the connection between beauty and Angel Clare in the novel.]

Hardy's wish to reveal beauty in ugliness in *Tess* is a major effort in characterization, especially in respect to his depiction of Angel Clare, a character much neglected, or, when not neglected, much maligned, by readers of the novel. Angel is often dismissed as incompletely realized, or as unattractive—to his author as well as to the reader. Some readers may feel that

Hardy does not satisfactorily account for Angel's tendency to live by stern moral scruples when sympathy would be the more merciful response to human suffering. Hardy's supposed difficulty in bringing Angel to life is sometimes attributed to Angel being a partial self-portrait, a figure on whom Hardy could not gain sufficient distance to portray convincingly.

On the other hand, when one considers Angel in the context of Hardy's effort to display the working of the beaugly, it is clear that Hardy sets up Angel to see in Tess, for the most compellingly intimate reasons, the beauty of defect, but then, finally, only ugliness, deficiency, and failure. That is, Angel is a study in thwarted sympathy, a study in hobbled imagination. He is interesting because he is haunted by some of the same questions we have been asking throughout this book: How can there be beauty in ugliness? Of what practical value is it to set aside moral judgment in the interest of beauty when faced with violence, death, cruelty, hatred, or other extreme circumstances? Is it not inhumane to even look for beauty in such events?

Hardy moves Angel through his inner debate first by portraying his abandonment of Tess after he discovers (on his wedding night) that Tess is not pure, then, second, by having Angel reason his way toward loving acceptance of Tess after long absence from her, and finally, by having him retract this acceptance upon discovering that Tess has renewed her relationship with Alec.

Perhaps the most revealing episode of Angel's overly thoughtful life occurs shortly after he has decided to abandon Tess, when, on his way to he knows not where, he unexpectedly meets Izz Huett, one of Tess's companions from Talbothays. Izz has long loved Angel, and Angel has been aware of her interest in him. For a moment, Angel flirts with the notion of taking up with Izz, of inviting her to accompany him on his travels: "[Clare] was incensed against his fate, bitterly disposed towards social ordinances; for they had cooped him up in a corner out of which there was no legitimate pathway. Why not be revenged on society by shaping his future domesticities loosely, instead of kissing the pedagogic rod of convention in this ensnaring manner?" Angel goes so far as to ask Izz to join him in his cart, and they drive together for two miles. Angel asks Izz if she loves him more than Tess does, to which Izz replies, "No, . . . not more than she. . . . Because nobody could love 'ee more than Tess did! . . . She would have laid down her life for 'ee. I could do no more!"

Izz's honesty about Tess's love causes Angel to turn back on his decision to make Izz his companion, and he does this at great pain to himself and even greater pain to poor Izz. But though renewed knowledge of Tess's extraordinary love for him prevents his "impulse toward folly and treachery," it does not turn him back to Tess, though he was "within a feather-weight's turn" of doing so. He has no "contempt for her nature, nor the probable state of her heart"; rather, it is his sense that "despite her love as corroborated by Izz's admission, the facts had not changed. If he was right at first, he was right now." His love for Tess, unlike Tess's love for him, is not strong enough to transform the ugly fact of her prior sexual experience. He cannot think of who Tess is because he cannot set aside what she has done.

At the root of this stubbornness is Angel's need to cling emotionally and socially to values and practices that he finds intellectually inadequate. He has set aside the supernatural aspects of Christian theology but, without being fully aware of it, he clings to some of the more mystical aspects of Christian morality, particularly the notion that sexual purity is an apex of virtue, especially female virtue: "With all his attempted independence of judgment this advanced and well-meaning young man, a sample product of the last five-and-twenty years, was yet the slave to custom and conventionality when surprised back to her early teachings." Once Angel has seen the stupidity in deserting Tess because she had borne a child out of wedlock, it should be simple for him to reunite with her, no matter what her circumstances. But he finds it impossible because his traditional feelings and tastes are stronger than his liberated ideas. He cannot find satisfaction in a woman whose condition he knows his family, with their stern sense of respectability, would deplore. Like them, "in considering what Tess was not he overlooked what she was, and forgot that the defective can be more than the entire."

So Hardy cannot plausibly portray Angel as capable of changing his mind about the possibility that beauty dwells where ugliness of moral defect lives, because then Angel would have to forget entirely his puritanical reason for rejecting Tess. For an idealist like Angel, forgiving is a humane ideal in its own right; forgetting, however, is something entirely different. He cannot forget Tess's past, cannot shake free of his obsession with "freshness" because, as Tess shrewdly tells him, "It is in your own mind, what you are angry at, Angel; it is not in me." Tess is only half right, for Angel is actually both angry about what Tess has done and victimized by the way he thinks.

—Peter J. Casagrande, Tess of the D'Urbervilles: *Unorthodox Beauty* (New York: Twayne, 1992), pp. 99–101

❖

BYRON CAMERINO-SANTANGELO ON MAN AND MACHINE IN *TESS OF THE D'URBERVILLES*

[Byron Camerino-Santangelo is a professor of English at the University of California at Irvine. In this extract, Camerino-Santangelo finds that the contrast between human beings and machinery is a central metaphor in *Tess*.]

In *Tess*, the blindness and arbitrariness of natural law indicate that it works mechanically and, significantly, the imagery of the novel often equates nature and technology. (Certainly, Hardy, unlike ⟨Thomas Henry⟩ Huxley, does not view science as a force which contributes to ethical progress.) This imagery portrays both as forces which blindly affect man, and which are neither subject to his will nor benevolent. Even at those moments when the narrator contrasts nature and industrial progress, his division between them does not hold up. When Tess and Angel take the milk from Talbothay's to the train station, the train is described as completely 'foreign' to the 'unsophisticated girl', whose attitude resembles that 'of a friendly leopard at pause.' However, the distinction between train and nature breaks down since the train itself is described in natural terms. It represents modern life stretching forth 'a steam feeler . . . three or four times a day', and then withdrawing this feeler 'as if what it touched had been uncongenial'. During the mid and late nineteenth century, railroads were a symbol of Britain's incredible industrial and economic growth. Thus, in *Tess* the train working like a blind tendril of a plant, adumbrates the forthcoming growth of the modern which will, like a weed, take over Tess' bucolic world.

In the threshing scene at Flintcomb-Ash, the similarity between natural and technological laws lies in their power over man's will. The threshing machine works blindly, like the productive and reproductive laws of nature. It is a 'red tyrant' which 'whilst it was going, kept up a despotic demand upon the endurance of the [women's] muscles and nerves.' The blind power of the machine is also represented by the steam engine which, like nature, propels and moves a world, but without awareness or sensitivity; it is 'the primum mobile of this little world'. The autonomous and formative power of the machine is emphasized by the figure of 'the engineman'. He is a new kind of man, alienated from the agricultural way of life: 'He was in the agricultural world, but not of it. He served fire and smoke; these denizens of the fields served vegetation, weather, frost, and sun.' The 'engineman' may have control over starting and stopping this machine, but the force of technology itself has control over his development; he now 'serves' different masters. Subservience for the workers is not simply defined as submission to those with economic control, but also as enslavement to the force of technology itself.

In *Tess,* mechanical progress runs parallel and contributes to the 'universal harshness' of the laws of nature which grind forward oblivious to human happiness, desire, and will. Contradicting his own notion of a benevolent natural structure, the narrator claims that these laws are the underlying cause of Tess's misery. For example, they only allow Angel and Tess to get together after it is too late:

> Nature does not often say 'See!' to her poor creature at a time when seeing can lead to happy doing; or reply 'Here' to a body's cry of 'Where?' till the hide-and-seek has become an irksome game.

The blind, mechanical operation of Tess's world prevents a proper order or direction from developing. If the universe had a logical order, intention and result would correspond, and compatible couples would meet at the right time. Human lives would make sense. 'Universal harshness' is the impossibility of finding a totalizing purpose which could give meaning to the series of events which make up a life; the temporal spaces between those events necessarily prevent them from unifying into an intelligible whole. This lack of unity creates 'the harshness of the means towards the aims, of today towards yesterday, of hereafter towards today.' Tess's life is one sad example of 'the harshness'. First her father learns of his heritage, then in celebration he becomes too drunk to take the bee-hives to market. Tess falls asleep on her unexpected trip with the hives and the family horse, Prince, is killed by the mailwagon; in atonement, Tess goes to seek the help of the new D'Urbervilles. At the Chase, an unfortunate series of incidents on market night leads to her rape by Alec, which, in turn, precipitates another series of events leading to her death. The sequence of Tess's life has a certain horrible inevitability, and yet there is no determining explanation which could make sense of it. Social injustice, nature, economic upheaval all offer partial explanations, but none of these factors can account entirely for Tess's horrible fate. In Hardy's *The Dynasts,* the spirits discuss the controlling force of the universe, the 'Immanent Will'. Like nature and society in *Tess,* the 'Will' works 'unconsciously'. It structures events with 'clocklike laws', but these laws have no controlling purpose. Only half awake: 'like a knitter drowsed, / whose fingers play in skilled unmindfulness. / The will has woven with an absent heed / Since life first was; and ever will so weave.' Hardy personifies the force which structures human lives as a being who works unceasingly, but without thought, much like the threshing machine. Thus, the structure it creates is senseless, and this senselessness is cruel since it takes no 'heed' of human intention or happiness. Hardy would certainly have agreed with Huxley that the 'cosmic process' necessarily conflicts with any 'ethical process'.

Tess herself cries out against the 'clock-like' universal laws which spawn her misery. Alec shows up at the threshing machine, and while Tess eats her lunch, he tries to convince her to come away with him. When Tess refuses, he grows angry and calls Angel a mule. In response, Tess hits him with a heavy gauntlet, drawing blood. Alec starts up, as if to strike her back, and Tess's rising and then sinking again, cries.

> 'Now, punish me! . . . 'Whip me, crush me; you need not mind those people under the rick! I shall not cry out. Once victim, always victim—that's the law!'

As I will show later, Tess is actually taunting Alec here, but her bitter summation of 'the law' is frightfully accurate in the context of the novel. In Hardy's portrayal of society, once a woman is violated by a man, she is perpetually made into 'victim' afterwards. 'The law' also seems to apply to the social and economic practices which dictate that those who do manual field labour are doomed to serve and be used by those with money and power; Tess and her family are victimized by landlords and by brutal masters like farmer Groby. However, social and economic practices can change, and Tess speaks of an immutable, universal law which dictates that some people will always be victims; Alec, farmer Groby, the bleak landscape of Flintcomb-Ash, and the threshing machine are only its manifestations. In her world, this law is particularly horrible because it has no intelligible purpose and its operative principles take into account neither a person's intent nor his or her character.

—Byron Camerino-Santangelo, "A Moral Dilemma: Ethics in *Tess of the D'Urbervilles,*" *English Studies* 75, No. 1 (January 1994): 53–55

❖

ELLEN LEW SPRECHMAN ON TESS AND HER BABY

[Ellen Lew Sprechman is a professor of English at Florida International University and the author of *Seeing Women as Men* (1995), a study of Hardy from which the following extract is taken. Here, Sprechman notes that Tess's treatment of her baby is one of the chief examples of her heroism and courage.]

We see in the character of Tess a wonderful example of ethical evolution. Coming as she does from simple, passive parents and a protected, innocent childhood, she could easily remain in this simple state. But circumstance (the seduction and resultant pregnancy) forces her out of her childhood lethargy. Virginia Hyman asserts that:

> Tess's moral development begins with her family's economic and social exploitation of her. Alec's sexual exploitation of her makes her more acutely aware of a sense of personal guilt. After the birth of her child, however, she becomes aware that such guilt has been induced by social convention and that 'most of her misery had been generated by her conventional aspect and not by her innate sensations.' As a result of this refining process, Tess loses the sense of a conventional social self and gains a sense of her own uniqueness.

Despite Tess's youth and seeming passivity, she exhibits at this time and at many times in the future, the strength to withstand outside pressure and to stand firm in her convictions. She makes decisions that undermine her own comfort and safety. She never takes the easy way out, but instead stands firm on her own moral course. She makes her first major decision in response to her mother urging that Tess convince Alec to marry her. This is a reasonable request for a mother to make (particularly a Victorian mother), and for most nineteenth-century women it is a course of action they would be likely to follow. Considering the morality of the time, marriage would be Tess's only salvation. Tess is well aware of what lies ahead of her—what ostracism, what hardships—and yet she refuses to see Alec. "Her poor foolish mother little knew her present feeling towards this man. . . . Hate him she did not quite; but he was dust and ashes to her, and even for her name's sake she scarcely wished to marry him." Even when her pregnancy is evident, Tess refuses to go to Alec for help. Although "she saw before her a long and stony highway which she had to tread, without aid, and with little sympathy," she carries on, showing a strength of character one would not have imagined on first meeting her. Yet, Tess continually surprises the reader with her fortitude and positive sense of self value.

One of Tess's most impressive, heroic acts of courage concerns her baby, aptly named Sorrow. After secluding herself for several months following his birth, she resolves to face the world again, "to be useful again—taste anew sweet independence at any price." She goes to work in fields with her baby, although "she was not an existence, an experience, a passion, a structure of sensations, to anyone but herself." She nurses the baby in the field where she works, ignored by all her former friends. Yet, despite her sadness and isolation, "some spirit . . . induced her to dress herself up nearly as she had formerly done." The feeling that she had done no wrong as well as the knowledge that she was needed in the fields made her strong, and "this was why she had borne herself with dignity, and had looked people calmly in the face at times, even when holding the baby in her arms."

But more trials lay before her, and the grief over her unfortunate situation is overshadowed by a new one, "which knew no social law." Her baby falls ill, and Tess is devastated. "The baby's offence against society in coming into the world was forgotten by the girl-mother; her soul's desire was to continue that offence by preserving the life of the child." When, despite all her efforts on the baby's behalf, his death seems imminent, another realization plunges her into misery—her baby had not been baptized, and would, therefore, not be assured its place in heaven. She frantically sends for the parson, who, knowing the circumstances of Sorrow's birth, refuses to come, and Tess despairs: "She thought of the child consigned to the nethermost corner of hell, as its double doom for lack of baptism and lack of legitimacy."

As she prays to God for pity for the baby, a new plan for salvation comes to her. "Ah! perhaps baby can be saved," she says, "Perhaps it will be just the same," and showing great heroism she undertakes to baptize him herself. As she lights a candle and gathers her little brothers and sisters around her, the flickering light has "a transfiguring effect upon the face which had been her undoing, showing it as a thing of immaculate beauty, with a touch of dignity which was almost regal." She opens the prayer book, and holding the baby in her arms, intones, "Sorrow, I baptize thee in the name of the Father, and of the Son, and of the Holy Ghost." She sprinkles him with water from the sink and tells the children to say "amen." Her face shines with a "glowing irradiation" and peace descends upon her. As expected, Sorrow soon dies, but "the calmness which had possessed Tess since the christening remained with her in the infant's loss." Jean Brooks notes that "the sign of the cross that marks the baby baptizes Tess as a suffering human being. Conception in sorrow, toil for daily bread, frailty, freedom of will and awareness of human alienation are to define the new-created woman in place of nobility human and divine and innocence lost." Tess's dignity and intrinsic nobility in the face of adversity illuminates, not only her face, but her soul. In earlier Victorian novels, Tess's situation would be a minor one: "a lower-class woman who loses her virginity before she marries; a woman who experiences sexual desire; a woman who bears and loves an illegitimate child . . . would have been an example to women of *what not* to be and do." But in Hardy's determined hands, Tess becomes a symbol of what one *should* do.

—Ellen Lew Sprechman, *Seeing Women as Men: Role Reversal in the Novels of Thomas Hardy* (Lanham, MD: University Press of America, 1995), pp. 90–92

❖

Books by
Thomas Hardy

Desperate Remedies. 1871. 3 vols.

Under the Greenwood Tree: A Rural Painting of the Dutch School. 1872. 2 vols.

A Pair of Blue Eyes. 1873. 3 vols.

Far from the Madding Crowd. 1874. 2 vols.

The Hand of Ethelberta: A Comedy in Chapters. 1876. 2 vols.

The Return of the Native. 1878. 3 vols.

The Mistress of the Farm. c. 1879.

Fellow-Townsmen. 1880.

The Trumpet-Major: A Tale. 1880. 3 vols.

A Laodicean; or, The Castle of the De Stancys: A Story of To-day. 1881. 3 vols.

Two on a Tower: A Romance. 1882. 3 vols.

The Romantic Adventures of a Milkmaid. 1883.

The Dorset Farm Labourer: Past and Present. c. 1884.

The Mayor of Casterbridge: The Life and Death of a Man of Character. 1886. 2 vols.

The Woodlanders. 1887. 3 vols.

Wessex Tales: Strange, Lively, and Commonplace. 1888. 2 vols.

A Group of Noble Dames. 1891.

Tess of the D'Urbervilles: A Pure Woman Faithfully Presented. 1891. 3 vols.

The Three Wayfarers. 1893.

Life's Little Ironies: A Set of Tales with Some Colloquial Sketches Entitled A Few Crusted Characters. 1894.

The Wessex Novels. 1895–96. 16 vols.

Jude the Obscure. 1896.

The Well-Beloved: A Sketch of a Temperament. 1897.

Wessex Poems and Other Verses. 1898.

Poems of the Past and the Present. 1902.

The Dynasts: A Drama of the Napoleonic Wars. 1904–08. 3 vols.

Select Poems of William Barnes (editor). 1908.

Time's Laughingstocks and Other Verses. 1909.

Works (Wessex Edition). 1912–31. 24 vols.

The Convergence of the Twain. 1912.

A Changed Man, The Waiting Supper, and Other Tales. 1913.

Song of the Soldiers. 1914.

Letters on the War. 1914.

Satires of Circumstance: Lyrics and Reveries, with Miscellaneous Pieces. 1914.

Before Marching and After. 1915.

The Oxen. 1915.

In Time of "The Breaking of Nations." 1916.

Domicilium. 1916, 1918.

To Shakespeare After Three Hundred Years. 1916.

Selected Poems. 1916.

"When I Weekly Knew." 1916.

England to Germany ⟨etc.⟩ 1917.

A Trampwoman's Tragedy. 1917.

A Call to National Service ⟨etc.⟩. 1917.

The Fiddler's Story ⟨etc.⟩. 1917.

Moments of Vision and Miscellaneous Verses. 1917.

⟨Appeal for Mrs. Allhusen's Canteens.⟩ 1918.

Jezreel ⟨etc.⟩ 1919.

Collected Poems. 1919.

"And Then There Was a Great Calm": 11 November 1918. 1921.

The Play of "Saint George." 1921.

Haunting Figures ⟨etc.⟩. 1922.

Late Lyrics and Earlier, with Many Other Verses. 1922.

The Famous Tragedy of the Queen of Cornwall. 1923.

Compassion: An Ode in Celebration of the Centenary of the Royal Society for the Prevention of Cruelty to Animals. 1924.

Winter Night in Woodland. 1925.

No Bell-Ringing: A Ballad of Durnover. 1925.

Life and Art. Ed. Ernest Brennecke, Jr. 1925.

Human Shows: Far Phantasies, Songs, and Trifles. 1925.

Address: Delivered on Laying the Commemoration Stone of the New Dorchester Grammar School. 1927.

Yuletide in a Younger World. 1927.

G. M.: A Reminiscence. 1927.

Christmas in the Elgin Room, British Museum: Early Last Century. 1927.

Short Stories. 1928.

Winter Words in Various Moods and Metres. 1928.

Old Mrs. Chundle. 1929.

An Indiscretion in the Life of an Heiress. 1934.

Selected Poems. Ed. G. M. Young. 1940.

Our Exploits at West Poley. Ed. Richard Little Purdy. 1952.

Letters. Ed. Carl J. Weber. 1954.

Notebooks and Some Letters from Julia Augusta Martin.
   Ed. Evelyn Hardy. 1955.

"Dearest Emmie": Thomas Hardy's Letters to His First Wife.
   Ed. Carl J. Weber. 1963.

Architectural Notebook. Ed. C. J. P. Beatty. 1966.

Thomas Hardy's Personal Writings: Prefaces, Literary Opinions,
   Reminiscences. Ed. Harold Orel. 1967.

One Rare Fair Woman: Thomas Hardy's Letters to Florence
   Henniker 1893–1922. Ed. Evelyn Hardy and F. B. Pinion.
   1972.

Literary Notes. Ed. Lennart A. Bjork. 1974. 1 vol. in 2 parts.

Complete Poems. Ed. James Gibson. 1976.

Collected Letters. Ed. Richard Little Purdy and Michael
   Millgate. 1978–88. 7 vols.

Personal Notebooks. Ed. Richard H. Taylor. 1978.

Complete Poetical Works. Ed. Samuel Hynes. 1982–95. 5 vols.

Literary Notebooks. Ed. Lennart A Bjork. 1985. 2 vols.

The Excluded and Collaborative Stories. Ed. Pamela Dalziel.
   1992.

Works about Thomas Hardy and *Tess of the D'Urbervilles*

Bernstein, Susan David. "Confessing and Editing: The Politics of Purity in Hardy's *Tess of the D'Urbervilles*." In *Virginal Sexuality and Textuality in Victorian Literature,* ed. Lloyd Davis. Albany: State University of New York Press, 1993, pp. 159–78.

Bloom, Harold, ed. *Thomas Hardy's* Tess of the D'Urbervilles. New York: Chelsea House, 1987.

Bonica, Charlotte. "Nature and Paganism in Hardy's *Tess of the D'Urbervilles*." *ELH* 49 (1982): 849–62.

Brown, Suzanne Hunter. " 'Tess' and *Tess:* An Experiment in Genre." *Modern Fiction Studies* 28 (1982): 25–44.

Casagrande, Peter J. *Unity in Hardy's Novels.* Lawrence: Regents Press of Kansas, 1982.

Collins, Deborah L. *Thomas Hardy and His God: A Liturgy of Unbelief.* Basingstoke, UK: Macmillan, 1990.

Dave, Jagdish Chandra. *The Human Predicament in Hardy's Novels.* London: Macmillan, 1993.

Davis, William A., Jr. "Hardy and the 'Deserted Wife' Question: The Failure of Law in *Tess of the D'Urbervilles*." *Colby Quarterly* 29 (1993): 5–19.

Egan, Joseph J. "The Fatal Suitor: Early Foreshadowings in *Tess of the D'Urbervilles*." *Tennessee Studies in Literature* 15 (1970): 161–64.

Garson, Marjorie. *Hardy's Fables of Integrity: Woman, Body, Text.* Oxford: Clarendon Press, 1991.

Gatrell, Simon. *Thomas Hardy and the Proper Study of Mankind.* Basingstoke, UK: Macmillan, 1993.

Goode, John. *Thomas Hardy: The Offensive Truth.* Oxford: Basil Blackwell, 1988.

Gose, Elliott B., Jr. "Psychic Evolution: Darwinism and Initiation in *Tess of the D'Urbervilles.*" *Nineteenth-Century Fiction* 18 (1963–64): 261–72.

Greenslade, William. "The Lure of Pedigree in *Tess of the D'Urbervilles.*" *Thomas Hardy Journal* 7 (1991): 103–15.

Guérard, Albert J. *Thomas Hardy: The Novels and Stories.* Cambridge, MA: Harvard University Press, 1949.

Hall, W. F. "Hawthorne, Shakespeare, and Tess: Hardy's Use of Allusion and Reference." *English Studies* 52 (1971): 533–42.

Herbert, Lucille. "Hardy's Views in *Tess of the D'Urbervilles.*" *ELH* 37 (1970): 77–94.

Higonnet, Margaret R., ed. *The Sense of Sex: Feminist Perspectives on Hardy.* Urbana: University of Illinois Press, 1993.

Horne, Lewis B. "The Darkening Sun of Tess Durbeyfield." *Texas Studies in Literature and Language* 13 (1970): 299–311.

Humma, John B. "Language and Disguise: The Imagery of Nature and Sex in *Tess.*" *South Atlantic Review* 54, No. 4 (November 1989): 63–83.

Ingham, Patricia. *Thomas Hardy.* New York: Harvester Wheatsheaf, 1989.

Kincaid, James. " 'You Did Not Come': Absence, Death and Eroticism in *Tess.*" In *Sex and Death in Victorian Literature,* ed. Regina Berreca. Bloomington: Indiana University Press, 1990, pp. 9–31.

Kramer, Dale. *Thomas Hardy: The Forms of Tragedy.* Detroit: Wayne State University Press, 1975.

Laird, J. T. *The Shaping of* Tess of the D'Urbervilles. Oxford: Oxford University Press, 1975.

———. "New Light on the Evolution of *Tess of the D'Urbervilles.*" *Review of English Studies* 31 (1980): 414–35.

Langbaum, Robert. *Thomas Hardy in Our Time.* New York: St. Martin's Press, 1995.

Millgate, Michael. *Thomas Hardy: A Biography.* New York: Random House, 1982.

Moore, Kevin Z. *The Descent of the Imagination: Postromantic Culture in the Later Novels of Thomas Hardy.* New York: New York University Press, 1990.

Morgan, Rosemarie. "Passive Victim? *Tess of the D'Urbervilles.*" *Thomas Hardy Journal* 5 (1989): 31–54.

————. *Women and Sexuality in the Novels of Thomas Hardy.* London: Routledge, 1988.

Morrison, Ronald D. "Reading and Restoration in *Tess of the D'Urbervilles.*" *Victorian Newsletter* No. 82 (Fall 1992): 27–35.

Nunokawa, Jeff. "Tess, Tourism, and the Spectacle of the Woman." In *Rewriting the Victorians,* ed. Linda M. Shires. New York: Routledge, 1992, pp. 70–86.

Otis, Laura. "Organic Memory: History, Bodies and Texts in *Tess of the D'Urbervilles.*" *Nineteenth-Century Studies* 8 (1994): 1–22.

Pettit, Charles P. C. *New Perspectives on Thomas Hardy.* New York: St. Martin's Press, 1994.

Rooney, Ellen. " 'A Little More Than Persuading': Tess and the Subject of Sexual Violence." In *Rape and Representation,* ed. Lynn A. Higgins and Brenda R. Silver. New York: Columbia University Press, 1991, pp. 86–114.

Sherman, G. W. *The Pessimism of Thomas Hardy.* Rutherford, NJ: Fairleigh Dickinson University Press, 1976.

Springer, Marlene. *Hardy's Use of Allusion.* Lawrence: University Press of Kansas, 1983.

Stave, Shirley A. *The Decline of the Goddess: Nature, Culture, and Women in Thomas Hardy's Fiction.* Westport, CT: Greenwood Press, 1995.

Taylor, Dennis. *Hardy's Literary Language and Victorian Philology.* Oxford: Clarendon Press, 1993.

Thompson, Charlotte. "Language and the Shape of Reality in *Tess.*" *ELH* 50 (1983): 729–62.

Thurley, Geoffrey. *The Psychology of Hardy's Novels.* Queensland, Australia: University of Queensland Press, 1975.

Waldoff, Leon. "Psychological Determinism in *Tess of the D'Urbervilles*." In *Critical Approaches to the Fiction of Thomas Hardy,* ed. Dale Kramer. London: Macmillan, 1979, pp. 135–54.

Wickens, G. Glen. " 'Sermons in Stones': The Return to Nature in *Tess of the D'Urbervilles*." *English Studies in Canada* 14 (1988): 184–203.

Widdowson, Peter. *Thomas Hardy: A Case-Study in the Sociology of Literature.* London: Routledge, 1989.

Williams, Mervyn. *A Preface to Hardy.* 2nd ed. London: Longman, 1993.

Wotton, George. *Thomas Hardy: Towards a Materialist Criticism.* Dublin: Gill & Macmillan, 1985.

Wright, T. R. *Hardy and the Erotic.* Basingstoke, UK: Macmillan, 1989.

Index of
Themes and Ideas

Date Due

Feb 28 2000			
Mar 15			
MAR 1 4 2003			

12165

823.8 Thomas Hardy's Tess
THO   of the d'Urbervilles